THE FUTURE
OF PHILOSOPHICAL THEOLOGY

THE
FUTURE
OF
PHILOSOPHICAL
THEOLOGY

edited by ROBERT A. EVANS

THE WESTMINSTER PRESS
Philadelphia

ISBN 0–664–20902–5

LIBRARY OF CONGRESS CATALOG CARD NO.
77–141196

PUBLISHED BY THE WESTMINSTER PRESS ®
PHILADELPHIA, PENNSYLVANIA

PRINTED IN THE UNITED STATES OF AMERICA

To Alice
for her vision

CONTENTS

PREFACE

"I have this fantasy," is a favorite phrase of a friend who is a psychiatrist. He uses the term not only in his practice but in his personal life as a preface to the declaration of his intuition. Fantasy is a vehicle for expressing his insights, expectations, and hopes—it articulates a vision.

"I had this fantasy" about the gathering of creative theologians and philosophers to participate in a "dialogical experience." The vision involved an encounter between theologians and philosophers where not only would programmatic proposals be made, but these proposals would be subject to immediate criticism, debate, and refinement in order to work out in constructive dialogue the most promising alternatives. The intention of this "consultative method" was to avoid the delay and frequent confusion of dialogue carried on by means of journals or books. The hope was that it would allow scholars to make direct contributions to and criticisms of their colleagues' positions during the period of formulation instead of responding to solidified proposals. The dream was that a man might plant a seed in another's mind or attempt to uproot a young plant already taking root—yet the growing season in this case would be unobservable. The products of such a dialogical encounter would remain largely unknown.

The envisionment, this projection of a hope, did not presuppose a clear consensus even about the direction of future theological conversation. Instead, the goal was thorough reflection and exchange to raise up themes or motifs that hold potential for being the most fruitful paths of exploration and development. The vision was of a consultation that would not lose contact with the ground of the culture from which it sprang, but actually influence theologizing, belief, and action.

Through the support and encouragement of the president and faculty of McCormick Theological Seminary, this fantasy became a reality. The Consultation on the Future of Philosophical Theology was held at McCormick Seminary on April 23 and 24, 1970. Twenty-six theologians and philosophers participated as Consultants in this dialogical encounter. Some 250 other guests of the Consultation attended the public lectures, observed the debates among the Consultants via closed-circuit television, and engaged one another in discussion. This book is the manifestation of that experience. It is, I think, something more than the remnant of another theological conference. This volume contains not only the programmatic essays which were grist for debate but, what is unusual, it also includes a report and reflection on the eruption of that debate. In fact, the dialogue is already injected into the public lectures themselves, particularly in the case of Heinrich Ott. This volume is the refraction of an encounter. The vision was for me partially realized, as the Introduction may suggest, for this resulted in a radical change in the direction of my own thought and work, although at the conclusion of the Consultation I was not aware of the process that had been initiated. It is my hope that even the mirroring of this encounter may be stimulating and useful for the theological reflection and response of others.

The four programmatic essays which were also delivered as public lectures at the Consultation by David B. Burrell, Van A. Harvey, Schubert M. Ogden, and Heinrich Ott are presented in this volume in essentially the form as well as in the order that engaged the Consultants. The sequence of the essays is maintained here not only because it is reflected in the concluding report but also because it provoked stimulating dialogue. The report of the dialogue is an ingenious reconstruction of the debate carried on in the four Consultants' discussion sessions, prepared by Donald M. Mathers, who served as the recorder for the Consultation. As Mathers declares, the report "does not claim to give a full account of the discussions . . . but it does hope to give a fair impression of the main lines of argument that emerged." The Introduction provided by the Chairman of the Consultation attempts to suggest a context and cultural contact for the themes and issues that may concern philosophical theologians in the future.

My debt to the contributors to this volume and my gratitude for their work and insight I hope is obvious. Thanks are also due to the students, faculty, board, and alumni of McCormick Theological Seminary and particularly to President Arthur R. McKay for making the Consultation possible. Appreciation is especially in order for the vision and work of the faculty committee on the Consultation: Lewis A. Briner, John E. Burkhart, and David Reeves. A special debt of thanks is owed to two other members of the committee, Thomas D. Parker and V. Bruce Rigdon, for special Socratic support and brotherly contributions to the editor. David Larrimore Holland translated the article of Heinrich Ott with patience and competence. Mrs. Deanette Small and Mrs. Deanna Eck carried the burden of the typing with grace and skill. My wife delayed two family holidays and while lovingly wrestling our two daughters typed, read, criticized, edited, and typed again. Through it all she kept her humor, humanity, and vision—what more can one say!

Finally, the credit for transforming this vision into an experience and enabling its manifestation belongs to those who invested their time and themselves in this dialogical encounter: the Consultants.

R.A.E.

Chicago

Consultants to the Consultation
on the Future
of Philosophical Theology

CARL J. ARMBRUSTER, S.J., Assistant Professor of Constructive Theology, Bellarmine School of Theology, Chicago, Illinois.

IAN G. BARBOUR, Professor of Religion and Physics, Carleton College, Northfield, Minnesota.

JOSEPH A. BRACKEN, S.J., Assistant Professor of Systematic Theology, Saint Mary of the Lake Seminary, Mundelein, Illinois.

JOHN E. BURKHART, Professor of Systematic Theology, McCormick Theological Seminary, Chicago, Illinois.

DAVID B. BURRELL, C.S.C., Assistant Professor in Philosophy, University of Notre Dame, Notre Dame, Indiana.

ANNE CARR, B.V.M., Instructor in Theology, Mundelein College, Chicago, Illinois.

DONALD D. EVANS, Professor of Philosophy, University of Toronto, Toronto, Ontario, Canada.

ROBERT A. EVANS, Assistant Professor of Philosophical Theology, McCormick Theological Seminary, Chicago, Illinois.

FREDERICK FERRÉ, Professor of Philosophy, Dickinson College, Carlisle, Pennsylvania.

JERRY H. GILL, Associate Professor of Philosophy, Florida Presbyterian College, St. Petersburg, Florida.

VAN A. HARVEY, Professor of Religious Thought, University of Pennsylvania, Philadelphia, Pennsylvania.

DALLAS M. HIGH, Associate Professor of Philosophy, University of Kentucky, Lexington, Kentucky.

ROBERT L. HORN, Associate Professor of Philosophy, Earlham College, Richmond, Indiana.

DONALD M. MATHERS, Professor of Systematic Theology, Queen's Theological College, Kingston, Ontario, Canada.

MARYELLEN MUCKENHIRN, Visiting Professor of Theology, Mundelein College, Chicago, Illinois.

THOMAS N. MUNSON, Professor of Philosophy, DePaul University, Chicago, Illinois.

KAI NIELSEN, Professor of Philosophy, New York University, New York, New York.

MICHAEL NOVAK, Associate Professor of Religious Studies, State University of New York at Old Westbury, Oyster Bay, New York.

SCHUBERT M. OGDEN, University Professor of Theology, University of Chicago, Divinity School, Chicago, Illinois.

THOMAS W. OGLETREE, Associate Professor of Constructive Theology, Chicago Theological Seminary, Chicago, Illinois.

HEINRICH OTT, Professor of Systematic Theology, University of Basel, Basel, Switzerland.

THOMAS D. PARKER, Assistant Professor of Systematic Theology, McCormick Theological Seminary, Chicago, Illinois.

JAMES F. ROSS, Professor of Philosophy, University of Pennsylvania, Philadelphia, Pennsylvania.

CHARLES E. SCOTT, Associate Professor of Philosophy, Vanderbilt University, Nashville, Tennessee.

FREDERICK SONTAG, Professor of Philosophy, Pomona College, Claremont, California.

PAUL M. VAN BUREN, Professor, Department of Religion, Temple University, Philadelphia, Pennsylvania.

THE FUTURE
OF PHILOSOPHICAL THEOLOGY

INTRODUCTION
The Future of Philosophical Theology and a Transformation of Consciousness
ROBERT A. EVANS

"I will pour out my spirit on all flesh . . . and your young men shall see visions." (Joel 2:28.)

Before we can respond to the query, What is the future of philosophical theology? we must deal with a prior and, I think, inescapable question which forms a contextual foundation for this discussion: Is the primal concern for philosophical theology today the justification of belief or the liberation of one for an experience that may result in that belief?

Philosophical theology has historically done the job of explanation and justification with notable competence. We have all profited from this effort and most theologians have contributed to this task. However, sometimes the quest for theological clarity has appeared to result in triviality. We have analyzed, dissected, qualified, and reduced not only our language about God but God himself. The mystery is eroded, the vision is corroded until God, or rather our experience of him, succumbs and God's demise is not only the result of a thousand qualifications but the impoverishment of a vision by which man lived. As Van A. Harvey warns, we cannot as theologians construct theological and metaphysical palaces in which we do not live. However, neither dare we make the building specifications on any theological dwelling so rigorous and so rigidly enforced that the only option is building a kennel in which no one wants to live. What we lack is the vision of a viable structure. In the words of Theodore Roszak, as he tries to articulate the insightful spirit of the young as they glimpse a vision of the future and seek to forge a counterculture, "We should reject the small souls who know how to be correct, and cleave to the great who know how to be wise." [1]

If philosophical theology is going to contribute to this vision, in which direction can we look? The theological student cries out in response, "What we need first is a change in consciousness." From students as well as from laymen and clergy comes the urgent plea for a form of theology that really affects a person's life-style. A theology linked to a transforming vision which affects one's values, his commitments and his expectations. A theology of illumination about which one could conceivably, in the words of posters plastered on student doors, "Give a Damn."

Such a change in consciousness as proposed here means much more for an individual than adopting a new theological position, such as swapping radical theology for a theology of hope and therefore moving from "contagious freedom" to "eschatological expectation." It means more than expressing a new theological vocabulary, acquiring the discipline of contemplation, or a decision to work in the political system again from a theological perspective. The transformation of the consciousness of a community such as the church involves more than releasing a few balloons in the sanctuary, experimenting with multimedia services, instituting personal encounter groups, or establishing a task force on national issues. Any of these activities could be symptomatic of being on the boundary of a new consciousness, but they are too often only adjustments to a different interpretation of the Christian faith.

A sensitized soul twitches under the present *Angst*, seeking a new form of consciousness. But even if this new sense of reality is desperately needed, how is a person or a community to formulate, create, or discover this new state? Where does one look for clues to this new life-style? What are the sources or intuitions for the type of engagements or experiences that might result in the reordering of a person's perspective on life? What are the marks of authentic futurity?

The attempt to grapple with these questions will, I think, elucidate the two theses of this essay. The first thesis is that if philosophical theology is to have a future meriting serious attention and scrutiny, it must be involved with a change in consciousness that does in fact alter one's life-style. The second thesis is that the most fruitful place to look for clues to this radical change in consciousness is in the instinctively correct intuitions of the emerging counterculture. This latter thesis may "blow your mind," because it runs counter to the traditional mode of doing philosophical theology. As Roszak, who has perhaps made the most comprehensive effort to identify the characteristic motifs of this culture, suggests, this fragile indistinct vision of the future is one of the few things "we have to hold against the final consolidation of a technocratic totalitarianism in which we find ourselves ingeniously adapted to an existence wholly estranged from everything that has ever made the life of man an interesting [and I would add, a humane and holy] adventure." [2]

What have these themes of the counterculture to do with philosophical theology? Or is this just another attempt to be faddish or worse yet to co-opt the vitality of the youth movement for the religious establishment and thus to have not a commercial but a "religious vulgarization" of the counterculture? This is, of course, a possibility for one barely past the mystical boundary of age thirty, leaping into counterculture senility, and for one who owes his soul to the company store of the theological establishment, a seminary. However, this is not the author's conscious intention. Rather, I am convinced that certain of these motifs emerging in the counterculture can be ignored by theologians and the church only at their own peril—peril of growing irrelevance and morbidity evidenced by sensitive people who confess that neither life in the church nor theological reflection speaks to their existential needs. Bluntly, we can and must learn from the youth culture. Even if much in this frantic experimentation with life-styles is bizarre and superficial, even if the Bohemian young are often formally, miserably educated (usually at our hands), even if we are confronted by an "adolescentization" of dissenting thought and culture, still their instincts are freer, more visionary, and instinctively healthier than those of us administering the technocracy.

These themes may turn out to be mistaken or inauthentic and only signs of adolescent rebellion and frustration—simply a more joyous cop-out than others of us who are frustrated with our existence could manage. Still, I am persuaded by the prevalent unrest yet persistent quest for vision among the young that these are the themes with which the philosophical theologians in at least the next decade must grapple. Margaret Mead contends that we are on the verge of a period when the young will "prefigure" culture for the rest of society. The day is past when one gained his culture from his elders, "postfigurative." We are nearing the end of the time when one received his culture from his peers, "cofigurative." [3] I doubt that the prefigurative state is upon us yet in the society and certainly not in the church, but if one is going to hazard predictions about the future, where is a more likely place to explore than with the young? It seems prudent to look among the students in the seminaries and university departments of religion who may be the future theologians and philosophers.

It might be agreed that it makes sense to look for signs of the future in the society of the young, but it seems questionable to direct attention to the counterculture which one must readily admit incorporates only a minority of the young and a few of their older mentors (outside agitators in a sense). The main thrust of the counterculture, as Roszak admits, excludes the conservative young who hold down lucrative establishment jobs or are frantically preparing for them in the multiversity. The militant black young, and increasingly the brown and red youth, are not in the movement either, but rather are struggling to reap the benefits of a technocracy that has prospered partially on their exploitation. Finally, the politically oriented, whether new left liberal, radical revolutionary, or Marxist organizer, feel estranged from the pacifist counterculture because their hope lies not primarily in a new mind-set but in a transfer of power. The concentration is on learning the techniques and methods of the present political process, of community organization, of guerrilla tactics, or of revolutionary propaganda and control.

Why, then, turn to the counterculture for clues to the future if they are such a minority? It should be made clear that those identifiable themes or motifs associated with the movement are certainly not confined to the young or to the United States, although the attitudes proposed seem to find their warmest reception here. Ironically enough, the expanded and redefined boundary of the "youth nation" is fourteen to thirty. That critical, almost mythical, upper limit will continue to creep up as those who, in some sense, initiated the movement continue to age, so that it will be transformed into a real "counter" culture, if it survives at all. More important, we turn to them not just because their number is multiplying but because they constitute what Herbert Marcuse has called the "Great Refusal." That is the rejection not just of national priorities, policy procedures, control of information, and authoritarian organization, but the great refusal of the present human consciousness and the values, communities, and actions that it yields. It throws an indignant finger in the face of a mind-set that is obsessed with and possessed by a consciousness of objectivity, rationality, individuality, nationality, secularity, and conformity. Even the repetition of the "itys" is as boring as the controlled efficiency of the computer, which has become the paradigm for the modern society. Some may say, "This is beside the theological point." Yet there are programs proposed—granted they are presently rare in such developed form—such as that of Dr. Herbert W. Richardson for a distinctively American theology. He suggests a "Christian sociotechnicism," where Christianity affirms and shapes a sociotechnical *intellectus* on the basis of "a recognition of its inevitability." [4] Rooted in American pragmatism, "the vision of a wholly artificial environment, man and society together restructured by the power of the machine, is the American dream." [5] This is a technocratic's vision (if that is an appropriate term) which can kill both physically and spiritually. The counterculture, in at least one of its characteristic moods, cries out against this mind-set, "Hell no, we won't go"—which refers to much more than just the war.

The counterculture embodies more than just negativism—more than just a refusal to cooperate with a process of dehumanization. There is a new vision taking form that is yet to be fully deciphered, but the major figures are emerging from the shadows. It is the vision of a transformed consciousness that emphasizes: (1) experience and subjective involvement, (2) recognition of mystery and the value of joyful creativity, (3) rebirth of authentic communication, (4) a sense of community with one's brothers, and (5) interpenetration of cultures and an openness to transcendence. This vision is composed of illuminating and transforming symbols that shape this consciousness. The discovered symbols interact with each other to create a new myth or drama which guides the shaping of a new life-style. It is these five themes and this quest for an illuminating vision with which I am convinced philosophical theology will grapple in the future and which I wish to interpret in this essay. The authors of the following essays and the Consultants whose views are presented in the report of the Consultation deal with various aspects of these themes. However, this is not done from the perspective of the counterculture as is proposed here. Nor am I implying of course that the contributors to this volume are inculpated for the conclusions I draw in reference to these themes. These essays and the Consultation which gave them birth was a stimulating dialogical experience precisely because new and divergent positions were ventured. This introduction is, I hope, germane precisely because it is an offspring of this experience, an experiment in thought which considers the possibility of one context for philosophical theology.

The influence of the counterculture, despite its minority status, is becoming more and more significant among the young and adult groups. Sometimes it emerges only in the superficial form of dress or lack of it, hair length, and vocabulary selection. There is even the danger of conformity to a new subculture not necessarily more authentic than the one rejected—as Tillich reminds us, everything has a demonic potential. Yet these signs are, I think, an indication of one's being on the edge of a transformation of consciousness. It is frequently our brightest, most creative, and most sensitive young people in the university, high school, and junior high who not only dress uniquely but express opinions that make the generation gap more than a cliché and play havoc with the expectations of the educational institutions. Yet the counterculture seems to intuit that real transformation must be wholistic. It involves more than a switch in apparel, language, and form of intoxicating substances consumed. It convinces more and more young people that they must separate themselves altogether from their inherited culture and move into communes or other experiential communities in order to work on the problem of consciousness and provide new models for this visionary future.

The fact is beginning to dawn on the young in their present suppressed and frustrated condition that the key not only to a "new congress" but to a new nation rests in the sphere of consciousness which is not fundamentally changed by another series of white or black papers or a few more antiwar congressmen. Harold D. Lasswell in his study *Politics: Who Gets What, When, How* says: "Constituted authority perpetuates itself by shaping the consciences of those who are born within its sphere of control. . . . Hence the great revolutions are in defiance of emotions which have been directed by nurses, teachers, guardians, and parents along 'accredited' channels of conscience." [6] The intuition of the counterculture is that you must give priority to a change in consciousness. If we wish to consider "conscience" a product of one's consciousness, then Michael Novak supports a similar point: "In order to take part in a revolution, therefore, a man must first do battle with his own instincts; he must first rupture his own conscience." [7] To do this means to expel or at least cull the old determinative symbols under which we operate. Perhaps that is why I like the expression of the youth culture, "blow your mind," because it suggests the initial process in the transformation of consciousness. The problem in some aspects of the counterculture is that the mind appears to have been blown clean without any replacement. Yet I believe there is a new vision emerging that has not been manufactured of whole cloth as the advertising images of the good life have or the great society created by technocratic culture. Quite to the contrary, the vision has been discovered or received as a consequence of reactivating sensibilities that were dormant and repressed.

The transformation of consciousness sought here could result in a vision of the richness, beauty, and capacity for human fulfillment in life. It fashions an alternative image of human identity, human community, and the modes of interaction between man and his world. The consequence of transformation of consciousness would be a new sense of reality. This new mode of experiencing is a metamorphosis of one's sensibilities, a transmutation of the valuational criteria, and a new way of adjudging human transactions.

This new image of man and of community is arising not simply as a consequence of man's experimentation and speculation, but as a result of man's transaction with a reality not apart from but beyond him. Perhaps one can be so bold as to suggest that the new vision emerges out of this encounter which is in fact between man and God. If this is so, perhaps one can even risk interpreting our present crisis as a time when the spirit of the Lord is being poured out and young men shall see visions.

The transformation of consciousness, it has been maintained, may become the focal concern of a significant and viable form of philosophical theology in the future. Several Consultants— Frederick Ferré, Michael Novak, Charles Scott—who were, in the main, advocates of the need for a new style of philosophical theology indicated that the idea of "consciousness" should be central in this project. The phenomena of religious experience require more careful scrutiny, description, and interpretation. It is my contention that a consideration of the themes prominent in that diverse phenomenon described as the counterculture may provide some very valuable clues to the future of philosophical theology. It is apparent that the motifs proposed here as emerging in the counterculture are not something "new under the sun." In fact, some of them are strikingly reminiscent of nineteenth-century romanticism and its rejection of the rationalistic bias of the Enlightenment, which was manifested in the "morality of knowledge." The rebirth of these motifs within the counterculture tends to recommend certain styles of philosophical theology as having the potential for transforming consciousness, while serious reservations are raised about the viability of other forms for the immediate future. A recognition of the pendulumlike nature of all theological and philosophical reflection plus the dynamic character of the historical process questions any long-term prediction about the shape of philosophical theology. However, tentative and short-term projections appear not only possible but necessary in order to establish themes and models that merit intensified consideration. To attempt to identify some of these was precisely the purpose of sponsoring a consultation on the subject.

1. PRIORITY OF EXPERIENCE AND SUBJECTIVE INVOLVEMENT

The renewed interest in data that is experiential in addition to that which is logical and theoretical is manifestly clear in virtually every discipline. Thus in theology too there is an emphasis on human experience as a formative factor in theology and as a starting point for reflection about religious faith. This is evidenced, for instance, by the revival of interest in Schleiermacher and his concern for "religious consciousness." Paul Tillich notes the recovery from the tendency of neo-orthodoxy to denigrate or discount human experience to a situation in present-day theology where it is impossible to avoid a discussion of Schleiermacher's "experiential method." [8] The call to experience sounds clearly from Karl Rahner's stress on experiential mystery, the heart of his theological anthropology, to Schubert Ogden's declaration of an "existential faith," the common faith of man without which it is impossible to exist. In fact, each of the authors contributing to this volume attributes an important role to human experience in doing philosophical theology. The pivotal question today is not whether experience will play a role but rather what role that will be and what mode of experience will be central. The issue raised by the counter-culture is the priority of experience and subjective involvement in determining one's life-style and for functioning as an adequate warrant for belief. Is experience really crucial in philosophical theology, or in the last analysis does the rational interpretation, explanation, and justification of that experience become the decisive factor? Or does the distinctively philosophical function involve supplying reasons for belief based on a "fully reflective understanding" of faith? Is its task to provide logical arguments, make appeals to publically verifiable evidence, and to inject all the appropriate qualification for statements of belief so that they will meet the criteria of the objective consciousness of the technocracy? If this is the case, then experience has no real priority, in the sense of cruciality or finality. What the counter-culture asserts we need is not simply a reconsideration of experiential data, as significant as that is, but a change in consciousness that appreciates the priority of that data.

"If you haven't tried it, don't knock it," is a colloquial way of expressing the priority of experience. The mind-set that this theme of the counterculture seeks to reject is "the myth of objective consciousness." Objectivity is the paramount value of the technocracy. Personal experience cannot be the basis for reliable knowledge because it is too susceptible to human error, to corrupting influence of personal feelings, desires, and expectations. What is reliable knowledge upon which one can found his decisions about belief, valuation, and life-style?

> The answer [for technocracy] is: reliable knowledge is knowledge that is scientifically sound, since science is that to which modern man refers for the definitive explication of reality. And what is it that characterizes scientific knowledge? The answer is: objectivity. Scientific knowledge is not just feeling or speculation or subjective ruminating. It is a verifiable description of reality that exists independent of any purely personal considerations. It is true . . . real . . . dependable. . . . It works.[9]

We depend on experts in this mind-set in virtually every compartment in our life because they have cultivated an objective consciousness. This is not easily acquired and takes intense training by "the disciplining of attention and selected habits of thought, the screening out of other sources of consciousness, control over emotions, and a commitment to private and public honesty, to care and precision, to technical statement and social cooperation." [10] Roszak and Novak maintain that we create a myth, a special conciousness, a sense of reality, which we find necessary to inculcate through our educational institutions. We work feverishly to convince students that this is what constitutes reliable knowledge and that decisions about matters of importance, determination of values, significant actions, style of life, even belief in God must have justifiable reasons that can be articulated and are at least theoretically subject to public confirmation.

This objective consciousness is ultimately at the core, I think, of what Harvey describes in his essay as "the morality of knowledge" which first found its expression in the eighteenth century, later was linked to the professional spheres of inquiry, and finally became educational policy for the university. It became incorporated in the scientific and technical mentality. One of its characteristic statements, cited by Harvey, is Clifford's declaration that "it is wrong, always, everywhere, and for anyone, to believe anything on insufficient evidence." [11] The issue here is what really constitutes "sufficient evidence." For this "morality of knowledge," technical reason is the final arbitrator as adjudged by logical precision and "shared warrants." Reliable knowing for Harvey, "is tied to consensus and social corroboration." [12]

This objective consciousness was sufficient and perhaps necessary for a child of the eighteenth century. The important question for the future of philosophical theology is whether it is sufficient for a child of the twentieth century. This attitude has "dominated the consciousness of the Western intellectual" since the Enlightenment, notes Harvey.[13] The counterculture declares that it is just this consciousness which needs to be transformed or at least is being radically called into question. The initial problem raised by this objective consciousness is that it appears to have too limited a view and appreciation of the human person. It leans toward a rationalistic conception of man that in failing to attribute comparable worth to man's feelings, intuition, and nonintellective capacities tends to diminish the life and experience of man himself. In this objective consciousness, man tends to assume the image of a computer in which one need only get all the proper information programmed and the direction of his life will be clear and secure even if it lacks vision and depth. At the root of what the counterculture believes to be a deficient technocratic consciousness is, I think, the idea that man makes his ethical decisions or reaches other life-changing judgments primarily or regularly according to principles or guidelines that have a rational undergirding and for which he can give evidence. We are becoming more and more aware that argumentation has very little to do with initial action. Rather, as Novak notes, "As the novelist well knows, men act chiefly under the psychic pressure of symbols, of images, of models; words, principles, and rationalizations come much later." [14] Those formative symbols and images are more a creation of man's nonintellective capacities than of his reason. We will return to the discussion of power of symbols under another theme, but the point here is that a transformation of consciousness, which would reflect a recognizable and more wholistic understanding of man, requires that the authentic priority of experience and of subjective involvement be recognized in any future philosophical or theological reflection.

Many young people are declaring that it is not the exclusion of the personal that makes knowledge reliable, that is, meaningful, but precisely the opposite is the case. Truth is subjectivity. Echoes of the Kierkegaardian theme are being heard more and more frequently in the counterculture. This is often interpreted as being antirational or antiintellectual. Yet the principal thrust of the critique of the counterculture is not antirational; it is instead antirationalistic. "The accusations are not attacks upon intelligence, accurate understanding or good judgment but upon the myth of objectivity as too narrow an expression of reason, which leaves out of consideration too many delicate but crucial operations of human intelligence." [15] Kierkegaard's use of subjectivity did not mean that there were no criteria for truth or falsity, right or wrong, depth or shallowness, but only that these could not be apprehended within the sphere of neutral objective analysis.[16]

This objective consciousness may be the ideal for the technician, yet it is in striking contrast to the philosophy of science espoused by some rather prominent scientists. Michael Polanyi has produced a most penetrating study of the personal role of the knower in science in his work *Personal Knowledge*.[17] He rejects the absolute dichotomy between "objectivity" in science and "subjectivity" in religion. He maintains that the scientist exercises personal judgment in the evaluation of evidence and in the selection of a given model or theory to guide further research. In a recent article, Polanyi has asserted further the subjective involvement of the scientist in what he calls the "dynamics of tacit knowing," which is kept moving by the combination of imagination and intuition, "imagination-cum-intuition." [18]

What possible direction does this motif of the rejection of objective consciousness as the basis of culture and the insistence on the priority of experience and subjective involvement indicate for the future of philosophical theology? First, it indicates that we perhaps need to move away from a theology of explanation and justification which insists on the priority of reason as the court of appeal either in the form of a new metaphysical vision of reality, or shared warrants for belief that are capable of public confirmation, or a hermeneutical interpretation that supplies an explanation of a faith in the terms of another discipline. Secondly, it means attempting to formulate a philosophical theology of illumination in which our theological reflection does not seek to exhaust by explanation the meaning of the theological symbols which empower and guide our sense of reality, our consciousness, our life-style. Nor would this theology of illumination attempt to justify our commitment to these particular symbols. Rather, this theology would employ intuitive-imaginative philosophical reflection in order to illuminate the symbols. It would liberate our sensibilities to a new symbolic consciousness. This illumination may occur via the function of a type of reason that includes the nonintellective capacities of man. This reason allows man to discover and envision symbols that are determinative for the fulfillment of human potential, able to expand our capacity to experience, and which facilitate more satisfying and creative transactions with our fellowmen and with God. Thirdly, it suggests that we need to develop a broader concept of reason and thought than is presently accepted in technocracy. It means that theology may need to look to figures such as Nietzsche, Kierkegaard, James, Bergson, the later Wittgenstein, and the later Heidegger, to men who recognized the boundaries of language, of objectivity, and of "technical thinking." Heidegger, for instance, rejects "technical" or "calculative" (*verrechnen*) thought as being an inadequate form of thought or reason.[19] He advocates a wider understanding of thought described as "essential" or "foundational" (*das wesentliche Denken*).[20] The characteristics of foundational thought are its receptive nature and its experiential quality. Philosophical theology if it is to effect a change of consciousness must emphasize a kind of reflection or thinking that does not involve man's objectively disposing of the subject matter from a position of distance, but rather grows out of an occurrence or event that happens to him. This is not establishing facts from a distance but instead is experience, encounter. However, for this encounter to occur, for the priority of experience, in this wider sense, and for subjective involvement to become a reality there must be something that is disclosed, yet something that cannot be fully comprehended and explained. This involves an idea of mystery and brings me to the second theme for consideration.

2. Recovery of Mystery and Restoration of Creativity

To be a humanizing influence is one of the primary concerns of the counterculture in reaction against what is believed to be the stifling and dehumanizing effect of the technocratic society. The criteria or even the model for what it means to be human is far from clear. However, intuitive appreciation of the mysterious and the stress on the free expression of one's feelings, particularly joy, which results in the restoration of creativity is at the heart of this vision of the human. The "joy kick" will, we hope, be with us for some time. But for joy really to have a "kick," for it to have a significant impact that changes one's consciousness, it must be more than the superficial "celebration of celebration." The basis for being celebrative and the source of the freedom to be creative perhaps lies in an appreciation of mystery.

The young have sought mystic experiences in part in order to find an alternative to the calculation, measuring, and manipulation of the establishment culture. As Lewis Mumford suggests, everything is routinized until it functions like clockwork. The clock is the "paragon of automatons," and automation is the key to the system,[21] so the young satirize this control of time by establishing communes that reject the significance of the system's time, or those of us who are more timid and still imprisoned by time, rather than freed from it, symbolize our rebellion by having big bright watches adorned by the countenance of Mickey Mouse or Spiro Agnew. But the yearning of the counterculture for a new sense of meaning and freedom is, I believe, authentic. These "neomystics," as Harvey Cox sees it, are on a quest for the holy and perhaps for God. Yet this quest is inseparable from their search for the human and is tied up with their search for an "authentically human style of life." [22] This hungry exploration for peace, both in the world and within one's self leads to a focus on contemplation. What is contemplation but a discipline to aid in achieving a particular state of consciousness? It is a receptivity to that which is revealed and fashions a total way of life. Cox suggests that there is a striking resemblance between contemplation and festivity because it frees us from the normal preoccupation with the routine for an immediate experience of "joy, appreciation, and anticipation." [23]

Often those who meditate and those who celebrate claim that drugs or liquor help. You can choose your side of the generation gap on that question. Despite the ambiguity of arguments about whether the use of psychedelic drugs means turning on or copping out, it will be a topic for the consideration of philosophical theologians in the future as it was in the past for William James, who experimented with nitrous oxide. In fact the reports of our students indicate that it is the topic in much of the youth culture now. Frederick Ferré raised the issue at the Consultation of the controlled use of drugs to aid or induce a mystical experience. The dangers and potential of this phenomena are yet to be fully examined, but what is evident to me is that one way or the other it will not be simply a peripheral issue concerning only the neomystics.

What implication does this recovery of mystery, freer expression of feeling, and restoration of creativity have for philosophical theology? First, there is already a recognition in theological circles of the "erosion of mystery" [24] and a kind of morbid fear, not only of the neomystics, since the church has always been unsettled by the mystics, to say nothing of the orgiastic neomystics, but fear of mystery itself, which seems vague and uncontrollable. Yet there is a sense of need in any future philosophical theology for a recovery of the sense of mystery and a linkage of that to the development of anthropology. John Carmody, S.J., in his glance at the future of theology asserts that a likely guide is Karl Rahner, who has suggested that "real humanity is impossible without a sense of mystery." [25] His emphasis on the intuitional aspects of man and the task of philosophical and theological reflection to keep experience and mystery in constant interaction point the way to a theology of illumination that highlights the role of the Holy Spirit. A spiritual, not a secular, theology appears to be a sign of the future.

Secondly, mystery is merged with wonder. The concentration on the liberation of feelings and particularly the expression of joy points beyond the dictum in our culture and colleges to suppress and hide our feelings and emotions toward what Sam Keen identifies as a Dionysian element in philosophy and theology.[26] Feelings and sensations are central in this theology which images "man the dancer," in contrast with "man the maker," in a life that is receptive and responsive, that swings with the spirit. This portends a philosophical theology less concerned with analytic scrutiny and definition of terms or the formulation of the rules for the use of language. Instead, this reflection would involve more concern with envisionment and elucidation of symbols, myths, and dramas that stimulate all the senses and thus affect one's consciousness. It might involve a different way of teaching philosophical theology or interpreting the fruit of one's illumination in a religious community (if that is possible). These new methods might involve techniques for engaging people in an encounter with the symbols of the faith, such as simulation games, poster art, folk songs, film, drama, and dance. The word cannot be dispensed with, but I think it must be allied with other forms of communication. It may become the task of philosophical theology to guide (not control) the selection of symbols and to provide interpretive depth by juxtaposing symbols that mutually illumine one another. In any case, in the context of this new celebrative mood it should be done freely and joyfully.

Thirdly, philosophical theology must strive for a methodology that does not so stress the task of representing insights in a systematic and conceptually precise way that it inhibits the creativity of those who work out and respond to philosophical theology. Many a student has been so overwhelmed with his first course in theology by all the delineation, detail, and drudgery that this experience decapitated any further interest in the subject. The student is often so oppressed with consuming and analyzing information that his natural instincts, emotions, and sensibilities are repressed until one is sympathetic with the theme of an essay entitled, "The Student as Nigger." [27]This does not mean doing sloppy work, but it does involve paying attention to the style of theology that allows a legitimate and important place for flights of the imagination, experimentation with myths and stories, and even bizarre illustrations. I mean an openness to the Spirit that inhibits our propensity for a thousand qualifications. It suggests a concern for philosophical sources that are more poetic and imaginative, even if on occasion obtuse. It calls also for a new sensitivity to the question of aesthetics and to the role of artistic imagination in envisioning myths and symbols with theological implications. Ogden reminds us in his essay that for Whitehead, "philosophy is mystical." [28] Its aim is "sheer disclosure." If one concurs with the sentiment of that declaration, then the motif of a recovery of mystery and restoration of creativity strikes one as an important theme for the future. An encounter with the mysterious raises the problem of communicating and interpreting this experience and the adequacy and inadequacy of words for that task.

3. Concern for Communication and the Symbolic Dimension

Heinrich Ott has suggested that communication stands at the very center of what it means to be human.[29] Yet human communication has an element of mystery about it. Communication is not the transfer of ideas but a "sharing" between speaker and hearer—a sharing of a mutual understanding about some aspect of reality. Our language provides access to or lights up a certain aspect of reality that is now available to both speaker and hearer through the medium of language.[30] Communication as a "shared understanding" has a context that is wider than the linguistic. However, there is a kind of focus on the problem of theological language that is likely to make it a prominent theme in any future development of philosophical theology. Each of the authors in this volume addresses himself to the issue in one way or another, and this is the special concern of David Burrell.

The notion of communication, of "rapping," and of getting through is almost an obsession with the young and particularly those in the counterculture. The lack of communication is said to result in a generation gap where one is alienated from his parents. However, the feeling goes beyond this in the counterculture where there is a sense of alienation as a condition at the core of human development. The young person is alienated from the established culture, from his environment, and even from himself, or at least the vision of the free self he desires to be. As Roszak reminds us, Herbert Marcuse and Norman O. Brown both agree that this fundamental form of alienation is primarily psychic and not sociological.[31] The power to overcome this sense of alienation rests with a change in consciousness. Thus Brown treats revolution exclusively in terms of an "apocalyptic illumination." [32] What is required is a therapeutic revolution that will transform consciousness and life-style. For the counter-culture, the guide to illumination is not research but vision.

The thesis I have offered is that the future of philosophical theology is linked to the transformation of consciousness. This alteration in mind-set, I maintain, is not initially or primarily affected by reasoned argumentation supported by evidence but rather by the reception of illuminating and transforming symbols. As Langdon Gilkey says, every religious symbol or myth entails a model of existence. "And since no culture can exist without forms of human excellence by which life is guided . . . even secular culture lives by its religious myths and images of man." [33] There is, then, particularly within the counterculture, a new concern for what I shall describe as a "symbolic consciousness." The "new consciousness" with which the counter-culture is preoccupied is the result of an interaction with experience. This experience, I suggest, is so affected by certain creative symbols that it could be described as symbolic consciousness. How does the symbol operate in this process? Rollo May asserts that symbols have two psychological functions. First, "they are man's way of expressing the quintessence of his experience—his way of seeing his life, his self-image, and his relations to the world of his fellow men and of nature." Secondly, they embody "the vital meaning of his experience." [34] It is symbols as they are woven into a story or myth that shape our consciousness and ultimately determine the way in which we act, our life-style.

How are symbols received? It is my contention that they become operative in and through a special level or dimension of language, namely the symbolic. The symbol ought to be understood as an "illuminating" and "transforming" linguistic sign which, due to its kinship with or participation in the thing symbolized, makes that thing or experience, through an awareness of it, present and manifest to those in a given community who understand and employ the symbol. This understanding of symbolism rests on a theory of the dimensional structure of language that cannot be developed here but for which I have argued at considerable length elsewhere.[35]

Because of the very nature of language in its interaction with experience, the symbol has the capacity to communicate authentic awareness and intuitive insight; it appeals to our symbolic consciousness and reorients our thought and life. The tragedy of the present situation, according to Rollo May, is not the consequence of a conflict between symbols but rather the absence or ineffectualness of cultural symbols. This, I believe, tends to produce a sense of alienation. Viable and powerful symbols have tended to disintegrate.[36] May's analysis appeared in 1959 but I think our situation is comparable in that man has tended to take on the image of a programmed automaton which adjusts to the routine demands of culture. What man lacks is a symbol or myth that would transform his life into creative and exciting adventure. What distinguishes our situation from that about which May as a psychoanalyst was writing is that we have hints that new symbols and myths are emerging. A new sensitivity to the symbolic dimension within the counterculture is a manifestation of the quest for and, I think, the promise of, a new appreciation of transforming and illuminating symbols that may emerge and very slowly be adopted by communities. I stress here the tentative nature of the prediction which is a strange mixture of intuition and hope.

Suppose this anticipatory sketch is not too wide of the mark. What might the role of philosophical theology be in this scene? First, I think it would be the task of philosophical theology to

envision and elucidate the symbols and visions which will transform our sense of reality, our consciousness. Novak, in his book
The Experience of Nothingness, follows May's analysis with the
declaration that what we require is a new myth. "We stand in
need of a new sense of reality, a new image of how to be intelligent, sensitive and free." [37] In terms of the need for new
symbols and myths, I think Novak is undoubtedly correct. My
difficulty with his proposal, if I understand it correctly, is that
man is to create or invent his symbols or myths. Man does,
according to Novak, continually invent the self. However, this
does not seem to be a very promising way of arriving at an
ultimately more authentic or humanizing symbol or myth than
we have at the present. Man tends to create that which he wishes
to believe. I would prefer to speak of discovering symbols. Transforming and illuminating symbols are the consequence of an
encounter, a transaction with that reality (Being) we call God
and which we confess to be the ground of our being.

The discovery of symbols founded on the idea that language
provides an access to reality seems to account more adequately
for the incredible wonder of communication and for the power
to change one's consciousness. Tillich reminds us that an
authentic symbol "cannot be created at will." [38] Rather, the
symbol is born out of experience, out of a "creative encounter
with reality." [39] Symbols are disclosed or revealed in and through
the symbolic dimension of language. This means that not only
the limitation and inadequacy of language is recognized but also
the power and adequacy of language as an event, an experience,
and particularly the transforming capacity of an authentic symbol. Tillich declares that there is always a dialectic of affirmation
and negation in regard to symbols.[40] The affirmative aspect is
the significant content it carries. The negative aspect is the
degree to which a symbol negates itself in order to point beyond
itself. Heidegger maintains that it is in language that Being
discloses itself.[41] It is my contention that this disclosure is in
and through the symbolic dimension of language, although

perhaps not there alone, particularly if one is to take the insight of the counterculture seriously. This means that philosophical theology must continue to struggle with the question of the nature and function of theological discourse. It must develop out of its encounter with the philosophical resources an understanding of the nature of language and especially of symbolism which is adequate to the wonder of communication and this new sensitivity to the symbolic consciousness. Philosophical and theological reflection, in order to capitalize on the power of language, should draw on the poetic and imaginative realm. To envision symbols it may be necessary to tell parables, unfold dramas, and paint pictures. As Sam Keen suggests, "Theological language is a way of giving form to those wondering moments when we find ourselves possessed by a power which makes life whole and holy." [42]

However, there is not only a Dionysian element in language but also an Apollonian element noted by Keen, and Nietzsche before him in *The Birth of Tragedy*.[43] To extend this metaphor, there is not only a symbolic dimension of language but there is also a conceptual dimension of language. It is in the conceptual dimension of language that the interpretation of the symbol occurs. Here we employ precise conceptual analysis, the standards of formal logic, and an appeal to evidence that can be confirmed within a given universe of discourse. There are two aspects of interpretation: (1) expansion that attempts to elucidate what the reality is to which the symbol refers, and (2) evaluation that is the attempt to determine its existential and ontological import. The important thrust is that expansion is not to be conceived as substitution. The symbol has the power to create or shape the consciousness in a way that cannot be replaced by information. The interpretation only liberates the reader to apprehend the symbol. For example, the work of the literary critic can never provide a substitute for an encounter with the poem or narrative.[44] His task is to facilitate our aesthetic experience with the work of art, to be open to the way in which the poem speaks. Nor is evaluation to be construed as the final judgment or court of appeal concerning the authenticity of the symbol to be transforming and illuminating. Rather, the process raises questions about whether the symbol is still alive and viable for the consciousness of a given community. Is the symbol "God" still a functioning reality or has it, as some theologians have on occasion proclaimed, died for the consciousness of the modern man? The process of evaluation cannot make the final judgment; only the experience of one's symbolic consciousness can provide the answer. The task of interpretation is to liberate and not to imprison the symbol. We must take care not to so dissect, analyze, and qualify the symbol that we debilitate its power and contribute to its demise. To adapt one of Roszak's images, the theologian must take care not to build such a sophisticated framework of thought that it is "rather like trying to graft an oak tree onto a wild flower. How to sustain the oak tree? More important, how to avoid crushing the wild flower." [45] It is my conviction that not only do these two dimensions of language, the symbolic and the conceptual, operate in every major universe of discourse but that these dimensions must be seen in their interdependence and dialectic relation.[46] The symbol needs interpretation by the conceptual. The conceptual requires symbolic insight. However, it should be emphasized that the priority belongs to the symbolic, linked to the experiential realm, which is capable of a transformation in consciousness. Whatever symbols emerge that do make life more humane, creative, and fulfilled will be understood by theologians as due to the gracious action of God and his transaction with man. Revelation is for me the source of transformation and illumination.

The concern for communication, and the symbolic consciousness which finally makes that possible, are significant themes for the counterculture and will become so, I believe, for philosophical theology where it is already prefigured. Cox declares that there are signs of a new age of fantasy which will place us on the "threshold of an exciting period of symbol formulation and myth creation." [47] We must be concerned with myths and symbols of God not only as "Being Itself" but also as a "Dancing God," [48] not only of Jesus Christ as "Expressive Being"[49] but also "Christ the Harlequin." [50]

4. THE REVITALIZATION OF COMMUNITY

The consciousness of alienation prevalent among the young is often attributed to a lack of communication. This fosters a desperate search for a sense of community. However, many of us at one time or another experience this feeling of isolation and separation from those we call "friends" and even from family members. This "solitariness," many in the counterculture claim, is the result of a cultural phenomenon labeled "phony individualism." This has produced a society composed of self-centered, highly competitive egos. Is it surprising that we are hesitant to reveal important concerns and strong emotions, even to our friends and spouses, to say nothing of general acquaintances, for instance in a so-called community such as the church? Is it surprising when most of life is constructed on the pattern of a huge "Diplomacy" game where you succeed at the cost of your opponent's error or failure? Any indiscretion makes us vulnerable and thus the culture socializes us not to get involved in other people's lives. Education is one long competitive war for grades, dormitory rooms, dating partners, and even study carols. Novak, and T. S. Eliot before him, suggests that "a cocktail party is the liturgical dramatization of our culture." [51] You move around the room as individual entities indulging in a little pleasant conversation but free to move on if it gets either too threatening or too boring. The cocktail party, which so many claim to hate and yet feel compelled to give or attend, is a mockery of community. It is the epitome of phony individualism because it produces a banal conformity on the lowest possible level. It thrives on superficial pleasantness, the avoidance of controversy, and inhibits any real sustained involvement and commitment of one to another. This is true because of an image of man that is ingrained in our consciousness. This image proclaims the uniqueness and individuality of man but in actuality it allows him to become an instrument or a tool to be employed in the fulfillment of personal desires. Even friendships are founded on the basis of needs and interests. But this is only an outgrowth of the procedure where man treats himself as a tool and founds his self-estimation on what he has accomplished rather than on what he is. The criterion for worth is doing, not being. There is no possibility for intrinsic self-worth. Thus man braces himself emotionally to be shot down for what he does. It is little wonder (pun intended) that we fail to trust each other, that we feel isolated and alienated.

The desire is to break away somehow from this insidious isolation in the midst of contact that Riesman describes in his study on *The Lonely Crowd* and Buber calls "mass or collective loneliness." [52] There is a frantic desire among the young for authentic revitalized community, for sharing in another person's life, for the cocreation of each other's identity. However, for communities to become a reality requires a new consciousness about who we are as persons; new symbols are demanded to actualize that transformed consciousness.

Paul Goodman's contribution to the counterculture has been his notion of Communitarianism which has influenced the new left's preoccupation with participatory democracy and the concern of the Bohemian, young and old, to withdraw to a commune.[53] Some ask, "What leads to such an irresponsible abandonment of society?" This is when that society commands neither your respect nor your commitment. When this same society presses in upon you to cut hair, control your language, contain your freedom, and possibly in Asia to curtail your life —why not cop out? Or is it really copping? Perhaps it is only the refusal to make an "intelligent compromise" which results in a teaching position, newspaper work, social service, or certain forms of political activism. Once you are merged with the society, then you become indistinguishable from its mind-set and life-force except for a little extra hair here or there. The alternative, to organize a community of persons you love and respect or think you might grow to, is perhaps a courageous and responsible act. If the purpose is to seek more viable models for community living where intrinsic human worth is recognized, enduring friendships are fostered, and creativity is encouraged, then this may involve what Buber calls, "pre-revolutionary structure-making." [54] However, to be fully responsible, to express a concern to humanize not only yourself but the society, the attempt must be made to transfer the model to the wider society when consciousness is transformed.

We are painfully aware that many experiments in communal living are pathetic, as perhaps the movie *Alice's Restaurant* portrayed with poignancy. Why do such communes often fail? Perhaps it is because they lack a vision or model that would enable one not only to believe in but to act on the assumption of intrinsic human worth, potential, and creativity. It is in relation to the need for a guide and stimulus to revitalize the notion of community that philosophical theology has a future role. Simply to reorganize or relocate a group of persons is no answer to the vacuity of community. The symbols that might provide an undergirding for the revivification of community must be experiential and intelligible. Community will never be an authentic symbol for the group until it is received as such. More complex and subtle explanations have no market value. Heinrich Ott is perhaps on the right communal track when he suggests that theology must rediscover the social dimension, must break with our individualistic ruminations and develop a "hermeneutics of society." [55] This would require a philosophical scrutiny of communal relations so one would be better able to intuit transforming symbols and cultivate illuminating ones. Cox proposes an image of the church as an "experimental community" which as a "metainstitution" would train people to fantasize. It would be a fertile field where new symbols can appear.[56] Perhaps the new symbol for our society with a changed consciousness in contradistinction to the cocktail party will not be, as some have proposed, a rock festival, a fiesta, or even a love-in. Perhaps it might be a liturgy in which the meanings of life—all of life in its sensuality and sacrality—will be thematized and symbolized: a liturgy that becomes truly the work of the people as they dramatize and fantasize in order to receive a new vision of what it means to be human. This no doubt sounds like the fantastic imaginings of a wild visionary without hope of actualization—and that is true, without a radical transformation of the liturgy and of our consciousness. But that is not beyond the capacity of him whom we confess to be the Lord of Life.

5. PENETRATION OF OTHER CULTURES AND OPENNESS TO TRANSCENDENCE

Finally, I wish to mention an additional theme with two aspects, both of which may affect the future of philosophical theology. One contribution of technocracy for which many in the counterculture are grateful is the opening up of Western culture via travel and modern communications to new and stimulating perspectives. Other cultures, particularly those of Asia, have penetrated the consciousness of the West and have had a disturbing but exciting influence, particularly upon the young. This statement must be greatly qualified, since we appear to be very tightly locked into the Western understanding except for a few punctures on the boundaries. This is concretely evidenced, I think, by the observation of Tom Munson that the Consultation limited itself almost exclusively to Western religion and Western philosophy. Burrell dips into the Buddhist tradition for a major illustration, and Ott draws on an example of an encounter of Heidegger with Japanese culture, but the concerns are predominately Western.

The young are beginning to call into question our general Western myopia. Those persons who have lived at least briefly in non-Western cultures, mainly through the courtesy of the Peace Corps or the Military, and those persons who have studied the literature of the East, albeit in translation, have been confronted with new ways of understanding self, mind, and community environment. They have discovered in other cultures, "emotional richness and maturity, powers of compassion, sensitivity and endurance" that surpass what we experience in the West.[57] This is particularly true with nontechnological or so-called underdeveloped countries of the world. This taste of international culture has provided the clues for a wider and richer concept of humanity. This means for philosophical theology that the future surely holds the promise and necessity of more intensive study in non-Western philosophy and religion. The provincialism of the West is often seen as coinciding with an intellectual and cultural imperialism, as a visiting theologian from India reminded me recently. We can no longer afford to deprive ourselves of the new insights and new approaches to old problems that a more intensive study of non-Western religions holds. The exclusivism of the Judeo-Christian tradition is being challenged particularly by the counterculture.

"What theologian has influenced your generation most?" I had the naïveté to ask a seminary middler recently. His answer was, "Alan Watts." While this response may not be representative, it is significant. The counterculture has found itself turned on by Eastern religions and particularly by Zen Buddhism. Some of the interest appears faddish and superficial, but much is quite genuine and relatively well informed. Courses in comparative religion are enormously popular. Those within the church appear delighted that the young are interested in religion, particularly the neomystics, which is a contrast with the atheistic stance of previous cultural revolutions. However, what troubles these same religious people is the rejection by the counterculture of the normal ecclesiastical route. It may be that this refusal cannot be accounted for simply as a desire to reject the establishment religion. Rather, the young may well perceive that the contemporary expression of faith which has been characteristic of the church and synagogue in the West has had too narrow a view of reality, too constricted a consciousness. The Western believer has been too short on vision and too long on bureaucracy. The church has been too oriented toward tools and institutions and not enough toward symbols and persons. In this way the counterculture has called into question the relevance of our form of worship and of theologizing, specifically in its capacity to affect life-style.

The recovery of transcendence is the theme of the most recent volume in the New Theology series. The openness to and concern for transcendence has been one of the charactristics of this religiously oriented counterculture. Marty and Peerman, the editors of this volume on transcendence, raise the question of the significance of the distinction between "biblical-kerygmatic transcendence and philosophical-experiential transcendence." [58] The consequences of this penetration of the Western consciousness by other cultures and the apparent openness to transcendence in every form may make that distinction of relatively small import. If, however, a gap exists, then philosophical theology may have the task of bridging that chasm with its renewed concern for the symbolic transformation of consciousness in the realm of the secular and the sacred.

Thus the themes on the horizon which I think will probably occupy the discipline of philosophical theology in the immediate future tend to advocate a philosophical theology characterized by illumination rather than explanation, by description not definition, and by interpretation not justification. It is a philosophical theology of symbolic illumination and transformation. Some of these themes are discussed in a prefigurative way in the programmatic essays and the report of the dialogue that follow. If your futuristic appetite has been whetted and the link to contemporary and emerging culture has been established, then this introduction will have served its purpose.

What themes are actually developed depends, of course, on radical openness to futurity and a God who encounters us in that sphere. Robert Neale notes in his work *In Praise of Play* that play is the proper expression of religion. This insight guards against the tendency to take our discussion of predictions about matters of faith with undue seriousness. Our reflection ought to be in Neale's sense of playful and joyful, open to encounter and surprise, for the posture of openness to surprise is vital to the religious consciousness and useful as preparation for perusing these essays.

There is, I believe, a meaningful future for philosophical theology. However, this position can be occupied by me only as an advocate of what could be called a new style philosophical theology. It must assume a form that transforms our consciousness and affects our life-style. This holds the promise of being a philosophical theology of symbolic illumination and transformation which is more experiential, emotional, mystical, communal, and above all visionary. In the motion picture version of Herb Gardner's play *A Thousand Clowns*, Murray is a rebel against conventional society, sensitive, compassionate, and imaginative, but also irascible. He is engaged in an argument with his brother, who is trying to convince Murray to "surrender" and become what he describes as one of the "dead" people. At one particularly frustrating point in the argument his brother cries out to Murray, "May God protect you from your visions." And we answer in chorus with Murray, "God forbid!"

NOTES

1. Theodore Roszak, *The Making of a Counter Culture* (Anchor Book, Doubleday & Company, Inc., 1969), p. 238.

2. *Ibid.*, p. xiii.

3. Margaret Mead, *Culture and Commitment: A Study of the Generation Gap* (Doubleday & Company, Inc., 1970).

4. Herbert W. Richardson, *Toward an American Theology* (Harper & Row, Publishers, Inc., 1967), p. 29.

5. *Ibid.*, p. 28.

6. Harold D. Lasswell, *Politics: Who Gets What, When, How* (Meridian Books, Inc., 1958), p. 42.

7. Michael Novak. *The Experience of Nothingness* (Harper & Row, Publishers, Inc., 1970), p. 108.

8. Paul Tillich, *Systematic Theology* (3 vols., 1951, 1957, 1963, The University of Chicago Press), Vol. I, p. 41.

9. Roszak, *op. cit.*, p. 208.

10. Novak, *Nothingness*, p. 37.

11. See Harvey, below, p. 119.

12. *Ibid.*, p. 125.

13. *Ibid.*, p. 118.

14. Michael Novak (ed.), *American Philosophy and the Future* (Charles Scribner's Sons, 1968), p. 10.

15. Novak, *Nothingness*, p. 36.

16. D. Z. Phillips, "Subjectivity and Religious Truth in Kierkegaard," in Jerry H. Gill (ed.), *Philosophy Today*, No. 2 (London: Macmillan & Co., Ltd., 1969), p. 113.

17. Michael Polanyi, *Personal Knowledge: Towards a Post-Critical Philosophy*. (The University of Chicago Press, 1959).

18. Michael Polanyi, "Sense-Giving and Sense-Reading," in Gill (ed.), *Philosophy Today*, No. 2, p. 306.

19. Martin Heidegger, *Was ist Metaphysik?* (Frankfurt: Klostermann, 1955), pp. 49–50.

20. *Ibid.*, p. 46.

21. Lewis Mumford, *The Myth of the Machine* (Harcourt, Brace & World, Inc., 1967), p. 286.

22. Harvey Cox, *The Feast of Fools* (Harvard University Press, 1970), p. 101.

23. *Ibid.*, p. 104.

24. Irene Marinoff, "The Erosion of the Mystery," in Martin E. Marty and Dean G. Peerman (eds.), *New Theology*, No. 7 (London: Macmillan & Co., Ltd., 1970), pp. 25–33.

25. John Carmody, S.J., "Karl Rahner: Theology of the Spiritual Life," in *ibid.*, p. 122.

26. Sam Keen, *Apology for Wonder* (Harper & Row, Publishers, Inc., 1969).

27. Jerry Farber, "The Student as Nigger," in *Los Angeles Free Press* (Underground Press Syndicate, n.d.).

28. See Ogden, below, p. 62.

29. See Ott, below, p. 166.

30. For an analysis of communication along similar lines, see William M. Urban, *Language and Reality* (The Macmillan Company, 1961),

Chapter VI, and John Macquarrie, God-Talk (London: SCM Press, Ltd., 1967), p. 74.

31. Roszak, op. cit., p. 95.

32. Cf. Norman O. Brown, Life Against Death (Wesleyan University Press, 1959).

33. Langdon Gilkey, Naming the Whirlwind: The Renewal of God-Language (The Bobbs-Merrill Company, Inc., 1969), p. 293.

34. Rollo May, "The Significance of Symbols," in Rollo May (ed.), Symbolism in Religion and Literature (George Braziller, Inc., 1959), p. 34.

35. Robert A. Evans, "A Theory of the Dimensional Structure of Language and Its Bearing Upon Theological Symbolism" (doctoral dissertation, Union Theological Seminary, N.Y., 1969).

36. May, loc. cit., p. 24.

37. Novak, Nothingness, p. 106.

38. Paul Tillich, "The Meaning and Justification of Religious Symbols," in Sidney Hook (ed.), Religious Experience and Truth (New York University Press, 1961), p. 4.

39. Paul Tillich, "Theology and Symbolism," in F. E. Johnson (ed.), Religious Symbolism (Harper & Brothers, 1955), p. 109.

40. Paul Tillich, Systematic Theology, Vol. I, p. 239, as well as numerous articles on symbolism.

41. Martin Heidegger, Platons Lehre von der Wahrheit. Mit einem Brief über den "Humanismus" (Bern: Francke, 1947), p. 53.

42. Sam Keen, "Manifesto for a Dionysian Theology," in Marty and Peerman (eds.), New Theology, No. 7, p. 98.

43. Frederick Nietzsche, The Birth of Tragedy and The Genealogy of Morals, tr. by Francis Golffing (Anchor Book, Doubleday & Company, Inc., 1956), p. 19.

44. See below, Burrell, pp. 90–91.

45. Roszak, op. cit., p. 41. It seems to me that this metaphor in Roszak can be used to raise the much more important issue of the whole possibility of metaphysics—whether it is possible for it to be constructive, in the sense of comprehensive, or analytic. This will undoubtedly be a continuing debate in the discipline.

46. A demonstration of this in reference to several representative universes of discourse, theology, history, and natural science is attempted in my "Theory of the Dimensional Structure of Language," Chapters VII to X.

47. Cox, op. cit., pp. 66–67.

48. See Sam Keen, To a Dancing God (Harper & Row, Publishers, Inc., 1970) and Robert E. Neale, In Praise of Play (Harper & Row, Publishers, Inc., 1969).

49. John Macquarrie, Principles of Christian Theology (Charles Scribner's Sons, 1966).

50. Cox, op. cit., Chapter 10.

51. Novak (ed.), American Philosophy, pp. 8–9.

52. David Riesman, The Lonely Crowd: A Study of the Changing

54   INTRODUCTION: A TRANSFORMATION OF CONSCIOUSNESS

American Character (Yale University Press, 1950), and Martin Buber, *Paths in Utopia* (Beacon Press, Inc., 1960), p. 14.

53. See Paul Goodman, *Drawing the Line* (Randon House, Inc., 1962), pp. 97–111. Implications drawn by Roszak, *op. cit.*, p. 185.

54. Buber, *op. cit.*, pp. 44–45.

55. See Ott, below, p. 163.

56. Cox, *op. cit.*, pp. 94–95.

57. Novak (ed.), *American Philosophy*, p. 7.

58. Marty and Peerman (eds.), *New Theology*, No. 7, p. 21.

1

The Task of Philosophical Theology
SCHUBERT M. OGDEN

If I speak here of the *task* of philosophical theology, this in
no way implies an unwillingness to discuss its future. My concern is simply to speak of its future in such a way as also to speak
of our present—it being the nature of a task that it is the point
where the future so impinges on the present as to become a
definite piece of work laying claim to our attention and effort.

I should also explain that this paper consists in four theses,
together with a minimum of development or elaboration of
each of the main points they respectively summarize. Since the
issue they are designed to explore is precisely the task of philosophical theology, the crucial thesis is the third, to which the
first two are ordered simply as essential presuppositions. By
this I mean that neither of these theses is developed as fully as,
given other aims, it could and should be developed, and that,
therefore, much of what is said in these parts of the paper is
particularly vulnerable to criticism. On the other hand, given
my own interest in the issue of philosophical theology, which,
I suspect, is not at all untypical, the fourth thesis and its
elaboration occupy a much larger part of the whole than might
otherwise be the case. But the fact of the matter is that my
concern with the issue before us is entirely that of a Christian
theologian struggling for greater clarity about his particular
task and responsibility, and I have been able to see only gain

in this being taken fully into account in my contribution to our discussion.

1. *To exist as a self at all is possible solely on the basis of faith, so that the statement, "Unless you believe, you shall not understand," is true in a sense not only of the Christian or of the religious believer but of every man simply as such.*

The import of this first thesis could be made fully clear only by a complete philosophical theology, which would consist for the most part simply in developing its manifold implications and presuppositions. Therefore, the important point now is not to anticipate such development, but to recognize the irreversible priority of faith in human existence. To exist in the characteristically human way is to exist by faith, for what is meant by "faith" is fundamentally that elevation of animal feeling and vitality to self-consciousness which constitutes the distinctively human mode of being.

In this connection, we may recall that an animal lacking in such self-consciousness nevertheless lives by what George Santayana calls "animal faith," meaning thereby the animal's instinctive confidence in its environment as permissive of its struggles to live and to reproduce its kind.[1] To speak here of "confidence" is, to be sure, to run the risks of anthropomorphism, and a phrase like "*instinctive* confidence" (or "*animal* faith") may, in view of what has just been said about the meaning of "faith," be plausibly regarded as a category mistake. But this should not obscure the fact that there is a significant continuity between the animal and the human levels of behavior. To live in either case is one and the same with accepting the larger setting of one's life and adjusting oneself to it. The difference in the human case, which, of course, is enormous, is that the acceptance and adjustment in question are not merely instinctive but are more or less self-conscious acts. Thus it has been well said that man not only lives his life but also leads it.[2]

Yet if this is so, if to live one's life humanly is to lead it self-consciously, and in that sense to live by faith, it is also true that man is in a unique sense the being who can understand. Actually, so to formulate the matter obscures an important overlapping or coincidence in the meanings of "faith" and "understanding." If, as has been stated, to exist by faith is fundamentally to accept one's life and its setting and to adjust oneself to them in a self-conscious way, faith itself, as already involving self-consciousness, is a mode of understanding. Hence it is indifferent whether we say that man as man exists solely on the basis of faith or say, rather, that he never exists except as the being who understands. But this in no way retracts the irreversible priority of faith which is the point of the first thesis. The mode of understanding which faith itself is or involves, or, as we may say, the understanding of faith, *genitivus subjectivus*, is always to be distinguished from, because it is irreversibly prior to, that different mode of understanding whereby faith itself may be understood, or, in other words, the understanding of faith, *genitivus objectivus*. The explanation of this difference is that man is more than merely animal not only in his understanding relation to himself and to the reality around about him but in his capacity to subject just such understanding to reflective analysis and interpretation of a higher order. Man, in short, not only understands but can understand that he understands—or, because "faith," too, is systematically ambiguous in the same general way, we may say that he not only believes but can believe that he believes.

There are alternative ways in which philosophers have given expression to this important difference—by distinguishing, as Whitehead does, for instance, between the "practical reason" which Ulysses shares with the foxes and the "theoretical reason" which Plato shares with the gods.[3] But, for our purposes here, it will be convenient to distinguish between the *existential* understanding or faith which is constitutive of human existence as such and the *reflective* understanding or faith whereby what is presented existentially can be re-presented in an express, the-

matic, and conceptually precise way. Given this distinction of
levels, we may do justice not only to the insight that "unless you *
believe (existentially), you shall not understand (reflectively),"
but also to the truth that existential faith itself belongs to the
distinctively human level of life, and so is a mode of understanding rather than mere animal feeling and vitality.

Obviously, this distinction also enables us to clarify the important question of the relation between faith and reason. In the
broad sense, "reason," like "understanding" or "self-consciousness," refers comprehensively to the distinctively human mode
of being, and so coincides in meaning with "faith" likewise
taken *lato sensu.* Insofar, however, as we follow the common
usage whereby "reason" is understood more strictly as referring
to *reflective* reason, while "faith" is taken to mean *existential*
faith, reason and faith are quite properly said to be different
and to be so related that faith always precedes reason, not vice
versa. The importance of saying this is that the essentially
derived and secondary function of reflective reasoning, whether
as the logical analysis of ideas or as the translogical assessment
of experiential evidence, is thereby clearly affirmed. The whole
life of man, including his reflective life, is based on his existential
faith, so that "reason" *stricto sensu,* or as referring to reflective
reason in its several different forms, can only be defined as "faith
seeking understanding," or, in R. G. Collingwood's variation on
Anselm's phrase, "faith cultivating itself." [4] One implication
of this is that there is a necessary limit to all attempts at rational
justification. The existential faith by which we live—which, in
fact, we ourselves essentially are—neither needs justification
nor can ever be justified. Rather, it is the very ground of justification, which pertains, therefore, to those re-presentations of
itself in reflection which it belongs to human reason to provide.[5]

One further precision that seems required is that "faith" as
it is used here is not intended in a persuasive or eulogistic sense.
For reasons both understandable and legitimate, "faith" is com-

monly taken to mean simply true or authentic faith, somewhat
as "worth" is taken to mean only good, or "value," exclusively
positive value. And yet the least reflection discloses that this
natural restriction of meaning can be and often is misleading as
to the full import of "faith" and its cognate terms. Even a false
or inauthentic faith, which we sometimes speak of as "unfaith,"
is not simply the absence of faith but faith itself in its negative
mode, rather as evil is the negative mode of worth, or disvalue
the negative mode of value. This explains why an animal lacking in self-consciousness, and thus incapable of believing in
the distinctively human way, likewise could not be said to
"disbelieve" in the sense of the word applicable to a man.
Accordingly, in affirming that man as such unavoidably lives
by faith, I am in no way affirming or implying that the faith
which constitutes our existence is necessarily authentic, and
still less do I mean that our re-presentations of such faith
through reflection must always be true. Rather, I am simply
pointing to the fundamental condition of the possibility of distinguishing faith as (existentially) authentic or inauthentic and
as (reflectively) true or false and am claiming that this very
condition is and only can be our basic existential faith itself.

2. *Philosophy in general is the fully reflective understanding
of the basic existential faith which is constitutive of human
existence.*

"Philosophy," Whitehead says, "is an attitude of mind toward
doctrines ignorantly entertained." [6] But, true as this is, it fails
to specify wherein the undertaking that is properly philosophy
differs from the generic "rationalism" that is the gift and the
task of human reflection. The *differentia specifica* of philosophy
is not in its being a reflective "attitude of mind" but in the
particular kind of "doctrines" toward which this attitude is
directed in the case of philosophical reflection. Such "doctrines," I maintain, are those comprised in our basic existential
faith as selves, although, naturally, they may very well be

"ignorantly entertained" in the sense that we do not yet hold them in mind with full self-consciousness of their meaning. Accordingly, insofar as philosophy may in any sense be called a "science," it can only be an absolutely basic and comprehensive science, which seeks just such a reflective understanding of the faith that grounds and encompasses the whole of our life and thought.

Yet philosophy is like all reflection in being by its very nature historical. This means not only that it is always done by men faced with the limitations and opportunities of particular cultural situations, but also that it can scarcely hope to attain its object except through critico-constructive discussion with the tradition of understanding in which that object is already directly or indirectly reflected. To be sure, any such discussion would be impossible but for the "preunderstanding" that is always given in existential faith itself. But, since the task of philosophy is to understand such existential faith at the level of full self-consciousness, in an express, thematic, and conceptually precise way, it can hardly afford to neglect the contributions to this task that are already expressed or implied in the whole tradition of human culture. This is Whitehead's point in answering the question, "Where is the evidence?" "The answer is evidently human experience as shared by civilized intercommunication. The expression of such evidence, so far as it is widely shared, is to be found in law, in moral and sociological habits, in literature and art as ministering to human satisfactions, in historical judgments on the rise and decay of social systems, and in science. It is also diffused throughout the meanings of words and linguistic expressions. Philosophy is a secondary activity. It meditates on this variety of expression." [7] Whitehead's answer suggests two further points of some importance: first, that the "evidence" which philosophy must attend to comprises nothing less than the whole of human life and culture; and, second, that the properly philosophical element in culture has relatively less evidential force than the other elements on which philosophy in the strict sense is always but the reflection. Whitehead himself makes this second point explicitly when he says that "philosophy must found itself upon the presuppositions and the interpretations of ordinary life. In our first approach to philosophy, learning should be banished. We should appeal to the simple-minded notions issuing from ordinary civilized social relations." [8]

It will be clear from what has already been said that philosophy necessarily has both a critical-analytic and a constructive-synthetic aspect or function. Insofar as its aim is the reflective understanding of our basic existential faith, or, as Whitehead puts it, the "elucidation" of "that ultimate, integral experience, unwarped by the sophistications of theory," [9] philosophy is unavoidably criticism and analysis, especially of language as expressive of human life and faith. And this, of course, is the justification for the widespread contemporary conviction that philosophy simply *is* the analysis of language. But, since even those who share this conviction recognize that philosophy's concern is different from philology's, because it is with the "depth grammar" of our language, and hence with disclosing the "tacit presuppositions" of our forms of speaking and with mapping their "logical frontiers," the claim is pertinent that "the impulse behind that concern is *metaphysical*, not linguistic." [10] In any case, the historical function of philosophical analysis and criticism (and no great philosopher has ever failed to perform that function) has always been for the sake of philosophy's controlling function of synthesis and construction. Precisely in meditating on the "variety of expression" which makes up the history of human life and culture, philosophy always has aimed, and quite properly should aim, to lay bare the faith by which every man exists simply as a man, together with the structure of reality as revealed to such faith. Thus, for all its value, the conception of philosophy as solely or mainly analysis is abstract and one-sided and must give way to the more inclusive conception represented by Whitehead: "Philosophy is the attempt to make manifest the fundamental evidence as to the nature of things. Upon the presupposition of this evidence, all understanding rests. A correctly verbalized philosophy mobilizes this basic experience which all premises presuppose. It makes the content of the human mind manageable; it adds meaning to fragmentary details; it discloses disjunctions and conjunctions, consistencies and inconsistencies. Philosophy is the criticism of abstractions which govern special modes of thought," and its aim is "sheer disclosure." "If you like to phrase it so, philosophy is mystical. For mysticism is direct insight into depths as yet unspoken. But the purpose of philosophy is to rationalize mysticism: not by explaining it away, but by the introduction of novel verbal characterizations, rationally co-ordinated." [11]

As it has developed historically, the one general task of philosophical understanding has been divided into any number of more special tasks. The reasons for this are not only the growing differentiation of human culture and the need for a division of labor even within philosophy, but also the inherently abstract character of human interest and reflection, which makes anything like a complete reflective understanding extremely difficult, if not impossible. A still more fundamental reason is that our existential faith itself is nothing utterly simple or lacking in complexity, but, at best, a unity-in-diversity or a structured whole involving several constitutive moments. In fact, one is tempted to say that we live not so much by faith as by faiths, by a number of basic beliefs whose exact relation to one another we may well discover to be an existential as well as a reflective problem. Thus, for example, there is the basic belief tacitly presupposed by our whole enterprise of scientific explanation as constituted by the various special sciences. This is the belief that the world of events of which we are part is so ordered that our experience of phenomena in the past and the present warrants our having certain expectations of the future. Or, to give another example, there is the belief underlying all our moral behavior and language that some course of action open to us ought to be followed and that it ought to be a course which, so far as possible, includes the realization rather than the frustration of the various vital interests affected by our action. These beliefs certainly are not the only ones that might be mentioned, and simply mentioning them is far from expressing an adequate understanding of their places in the faith by which we live. But it may at least make clear why special inquiries like the philosophy of science and the philosophy of morals (or, better, moral philosophy or ethics) have been implicit in philosophical reflection right from the start and were bound to emerge as special disciplines given a requisite differentiation of culture and specialization of labor. It may also suggest that a similar explanation is to be sought for such other inquiries as the philosophy of art, the philosophy of law, and the philosophy of religion—to mention only a few that might need to be considered.

Yet there is reason to hold that the philosophies of science, art, law, religion, etc., are peripheral philosophical disciplines and are important, in the final analysis, only in relation to philosophy's central task of metaphysics. This is not the place to develop the concept of metaphysics so as to do justice both to its long and diverse history and to all it might be reconceived to mean, assuming the conception of philosophy in general as the reflective understanding of the common faith of mankind. But this much, at least, may be said.

Historically, metaphysics has been conceived from its beginnings as the noncompressible core of philosophy, understood as an absolutely basic and comprehensive science. As such, it eventually came to be differentiated into *metaphysica generalis,* or ontology, which is the understanding of the completely general features of reality, and *metaphysica specialis,* as comprising psychology, cosmology, and philosophical (or "natural") theology, which are devoted respectively to understanding the three basic realities of the self, the world, and God. Needless to say, this conception of the exact scope and content of meta-physics reflects the material metaphysical conclusions of the main tradition of Western philosophy. But, even in the case of philosophies which reject these conclusions—which deny, say, that God is ultimately real, or else so radically reinterpret what "God" means that philosophical theology is in effect reduced to cosmology or psychology—the essential structure of meta-physical inquiry may still be readily discerned. It invariably involves the most basic and comprehensive questions that can occur to the human mind, and the procedure it follows in answering these questions always involves some form or other of what I, at least, would be willing to call the "transcendental" method, by which I mean, in general, the raising to full self-consciousness of the basic beliefs that are the condition of the possibility of our existing or understanding at all. In other words, metaphysics is the vital center of the entire critico-constructive undertaking which is philosophical reflection. It is for its sake, ultimately, that all the special philosophical inquiries exist, for they are really so many contributions to its one central task to reflect on the faith by which we live and in this way to understand the nature of reality as disclosed to that faith.

To avoid misunderstanding, I would add that I have no intention here of presenting anything like an exhaustive analysis of "philosophy." Nothing at all has been said about such important philosophical disciplines as logic and epistemology, and there has been no attempt whatever at a systematic classification in which all of the disciplines could be assigned their proper places. Since any such classification seems bound to be incomplete and more or less arbitrary, there is probably limited value in trying to work one out. Nevertheless, if the understanding of philosophy proposed here is at all correct, it should be possible on its basis to give a plausible account of all the forms of philosophical reflection and to classify them systematically in a way that is at least as valuable as any other. My hunch, which is hardly more than that, is that this can in fact be done, and in such a manner as to offer a convincing confirmation of the second thesis. But actually doing it must be left to another occasion.

3. *The task of philosophical theology, which is integral to philosophy's central task as metaphysics, is so to understand our common faith as to answer the basic question of the reality of God.*

It seems clear enough that the question of the reality of God first arises within the particular field of life and culture that is commonly distinguished as "religion." To be sure, we shall soon see that so basic a concept as "God," precisely as understood by religion (at least in certain of its forms), is bound to have a much broader basis than religion alone could possibly account for. But we shall hardly wish to question that it is as a religious concept that "God" is first made explicit and that its religious use is and remains its primary use. Even so, to those of us who stand within the predominantly theistic religious tradition of the West, it may still seem strange to say that it is within religion that the reality of God first becomes a question. Is it not the case, rather, that God's reality is the ultimate presupposition of religion, that "God" is its "constitutive concept," analogous, say, to the concept of "physical object" in science or of "obligation" in morality? [12] For *theistic* religion, that certainly is the case, as any philosophical analysis of its "form of life" will readily confirm. And yet the concept of "nontheistic religion" is not on the face of it self-contradictory and does in fact seem to be illustrated several times over among the phenomena studied by the historian of religions. Moreover, even among the religions which are in a broad sense "theistic," for which in one way or another "God" *is* a "constitutive concept," there is sufficient variety to require the familiar typologies distinguishing between polytheism, henotheism, and monotheism, pantheism, deism, and theism, etc. To this extent, the reality of God is already a question for religion itself, as the question both how the concept "God" is to be understood and whether on some understanding it refers to anything ultimately real. How much more, then, must it be a question for a properly conceived philosophy of religion, which refuses to restrict its evidence to anything less than the whole of man's religious faith and life.

In reflecting on this evidence, however, the philosopher of religion can hardly fail to be struck by an essential difference between all that is specifically religious and the other fields of human life and culture. Unlike science, art, morality, and politics, religion cannot be adequately accounted for as simply one more "form of life" among several others. For all the obvious specificity of its beliefs, rites, and social organizations, it presents itself as having to do with the ultimate basis of man's entire existence and, therefore, as fundamental to, not merely coordinate with, all the other cultural fields. In other words, religion in general is the primary and most direct reflection of the basic existential faith that constitutes human existence. Although its doctrines, for instance, have their origin in a quite particular occasion of insight (or, as we may also say, in a "special revelation"), they are invariably put forward as having a general application and, in the case of the great world religions, as being universally valid. This is why Whitehead observes that "the doctrines of rational religion aim at being that metaphysics which can be derived from the supernormal experience of mankind in its moments of finest insight." [13] But, if the doctrines of developed religion aim at being metaphysics, the question of God's reality, which religion poses for philosophical understanding, is in its logic a metaphysical question. This is amply confirmed by the concept of "God" itself, particularly as it finally emerges from the immanent developments of religious history. Where God is conceived radically, as in monotheistic religions such as Judaism and Christianity, he is clearly understood as metaphysically real, and so as not even possibly the object of strictly empirical modes of knowledge. As "the Father

Almighty, Maker of heaven and earth, and of all things visible and invisible," he is understood to be the ultimate creative ground of anything that is so much as even possible, and hence to be in the strictest sense necessary, not merely a being among others, but in some way "being-itself." In fact, the God of theism in its most fully developed forms is the one metaphysical individual, the sole being whose individuality is constitutive of reality as such and who, therefore, is the inclusive object of all our faith and understanding.

This explains, of course, why philosophical theology has been traditionally understood as one of the subdisciplines of metaphysics. Because "God" is the metaphysical concept par excellence, the question of how this concept is to be understood and whether it refers to anything real can only be answered as a metaphysical question. The same reason, however, requires us to recognize a definite limitation in the traditional distinctions between *metaphysica generalis* and *metaphysica specialis* and between the three subdisciplines of which the second is held to be comprised. Although it may be useful for some purposes to distinguish ontology as the elucidation of strictly general features of reality, or categories, the fact remains that the God of radical theism is himself conceived as categorial, the one individual whose being and function are themselves strictly general. Consequently, if theism is true, God cannot be regarded as a third "special" object along with the self and the world, and ontology itself must be theology, even as theology must be ontology. Furthermore, on a theistic view, neither the self nor the world is a metaphysical individual in the same sense as God is. To be sure, for a neoclassical theism such as I should defend, the world definitely is metaphysical, insofar as the reality of *some* world is no mere contingent fact but is a strictly general, and so necessary, feature of reality as such. But by "world," properly speaking, we refer not to *an* individual but to a *collection* of individuals, which is more than a mere collection without order or integrity thanks only to the universal immanence of God, and its immanence in him, as its sole ultimate ground and end. By "self," on the other hand, we do indeed refer to an individual that is unlike the world in being a concrete, integrated whole of reality, and to this extent an image or analogy of God himself. And yet the self is no more than God's image or analogy because its individuality, unlike his, is not metaphysical, in the sense of being ultimately constitutive of reality itself. True, the self is constitutive of our *understanding* of reality, insofar as it is in its basic existential faith alone that reality so presents itself that it can be understood, whether directly or reflexively. To this extent, therefore, the self is an object of metaphysical reflection; and psychology (or, as we would no doubt say today, anthropology) is an integral metaphysical task along with theology and cosmology—as is evident from the fact that the self's denial of its own existence shares in the inescapable self-contradiction of all denials of metaphysical truth. Even so, the theistic view of the matter is that it belongs to the self's own essential self-affirmation to distinguish both itself and the world as but fragmentary parts of the one integral whole, whose individuality alone suffices to constitute the very being of reality as such. Thus Charles Hartshorne only states the obvious point of any radical theism when he says that "the import of the word 'God' is no mere special meaning in our language, but the soul of significance in general, for it refers to the Life in and for which all things live." And he draws the correct implication for the question of God which philosophical theology has to answer: "The theistic question . . . is not one more question, even the most important one. It is, on the fundamental level, and when all its implications are taken into account, the sole question. . . . Philosophy as a nonempirical study has no other subject matter." [14]

Strictly speaking, of course, there could be no philosophical theology at all unless theism in some form (including, perhaps, pantheism and deism, as well as theism proper) were metaphysically true. But this is simply to say that the alterna-

tive to a metaphysics that answers the question of God affirmatively, which, on my view, is all that "philosophical theology"
can properly mean, is another metaphysics that answers it
negatively—in short, an atheistic metaphysics. Since the question
of God is by its very nature metaphysical, it cannot be answered
one way or the other except metaphysically, by showing tran-
scendentally that God either is or is not the inclusive object of
all our faith and understanding, and hence is necessarily
affirmed or necessarily denied by whatever we believe or understand. Because a positivistic philosophy that denies the meaning of metaphysical assertions thereby answers this question,
it is itself metaphysical, and atheistically so at that. For, if metaphysics were impossible, God would be impossible, and this
could be so only if the faith by which we exist, and so our
metaphysics as well, were by their very nature atheistic. But it
is just as true that no metaphysics can fail to answer the
theistic question either affirmatively or negatively. As Hartshorne
puts it, "Neutrality as to God means no metaphysics," for "if
metaphysics knows anything, it must either know God, or know
that the idea of God is meaningless." [15] Here it should be kept
in mind that metaphysical understanding, like human reflection
generally, moves between the two extremes of vagueness as to
its meanings and recognition of their incoherence, with one
another or with experience. Hence, while there may very well
be a "metaphysics" that is neutral on the question of God, this
is only because its meanings are so indefinite that it does not
really know anything, and so is hardly metaphysics after all.

It follows from the strictly metaphysical character of the
question of God that any argument for, or proof of, God's
reality, as well as, of course, any counterargument or disproof,
can only be metaphysical. Hence the traditional distinction between theistic proofs as either a priori or a posteriori is at best
misleading and ought to be abandoned. This is not to say, however, that the so-called "ontological argument" is the only valid
argument for God's existence. To the contrary, since the concept

of God as itself metaphysical or nothing both implies and is
implied by all other metaphysical concepts, not only it but any
strictly general concept whatever (actuality, possibility, order,
truth, value) can provide the premise of a valid theistic proof,
unless theism itself is metaphysically false. And that it is false
could only be shown by the same kind of argument, to the
effect that any and all of our most basic ideas, including the idea
of God, make the existence of God impossible, and that, in the
final analysis, because the faith by which we live is in its essence
atheistic. Thus there is no complete list, to be made out in
advance, of all the possible proofs and disproofs of theism. All
we can be certain of is that any properly metaphysical concept,
assertion, or chain of reasoning will of necessity have theistic or
atheistic implications.

As to the place of proof in philosophical theology, the important point is the essentially derived and secondary function
of all reflective understanding, and so, a fortiori, of all rational
argument. Whitehead comments that " 'proof,' in the strict
sense of that term, [is] a feeble, second-rate procedure." He does
not mean by this that strict rational argument has no place at
all in philosophy, for he goes on to say that " 'proof' is one of
the routes by which self-evidence is often obtained." Thus he
concludes: "Proofs are the tools for the extension of our imperfect self-evidence. They presuppose some clarity; and they
also presuppose that this clarity represents an imperfect penetration into our dim recognition of the world around—the world
of fact, the world of possibility, the world as valued, the world
as purposed." [16] Here, it seems to me, is the charter for a
philosophical theology that neither overestimates the importance
of rational argument for God's existence, as is the wont of the
philosophia perennis, nor simply eliminates such argument, as
has so often been done by Protestant theologians since Schleiermacher. The truth cannot lie either in making everything depend on "demonstration" or else in dismissing proof altogether
in favor of "insight" and "phenomenological description." The

truth, rather, is that "proofs must rest upon insights," [17] or, as we may also say, all proofs are but the reflection of existential faith, and so essentially secondary, although for the same reason still important.

In any case, philosophical theology or theistic metaphysics comprises considerably more than the development of "proofs" in the strict sense of that word. The burden of its task, indeed, consists in two main responsibilities that respectively precede and follow any such development.

Its first responsibility, as Antony Flew puts it, is "to begin right from the beginning, with a presentation and examination of the notion of God." [18] This requires, in turn, that it seek to answer two fundamental questions: (1) as to the bases in our common existential faith for our having any notion of God at all; and (2) as to how that notion may be conceived precisely enough to avoid vagueness, while yet avoiding incoherence, either with itself or with our other general conceptions and experience. These two questions are so fundamental that no philosophical theology failing to deal with them could possibly accomplish its task. But they have a particular pertinence and force in our present cultural situation, for which the very notion of God is the problem, either because it is thought to be insufficiently based in our common experience, or because it is held to be incoherent both with itself and with other essential items of our understanding and belief. Ours, in a word, is a "postcritical" situation which demands that theistic metaphysics begin from the beginning with nothing less than "a methodical-systematic laying of foundations." [19] To ignore this demand by proceeding at once to develop the traditional theistic proofs is to guarantee that philosophical theology itself will be ignored by the one segment of society that has both the competence and the vocation to assess its claims.

And yet not even the laying of foundations for its superstructure of rational argumentation exhausts philosophical theology's task. It has the further responsibility, as Flew puts it, of assessing the "credentials" submitted by "the various candidate systems of revelation" that advance their special claims on a theistic basis.[20] Even if it belongs to religion by its very nature to advance such special claims, the fact that it presents them as generally applicable and, in some cases, universally valid means that there have to be at least some reasons correspondingly general or universal for accepting them, if their acceptance is to be at all rationally motivated. It is not surprising, therefore, that the great world religions have commonly adduced such reasons—in the case of traditional Christianity, for example, by way of proofs of miracles and of the fulfillment of prophecy and other arguments designed to establish the unique inspiration and authority of the church. Since these reasons are offered as exactly that, as reasons, philosophical theology has both the right and the responsibility to assess their logical and experiential force. Nor can there be any limit to this right and responsibility short of the necessary limit of all attempts at rational justification. So far as any belief or assertion, even a doctrine of religion originating in special revelation, lays claim to universal validity or truth, it both warrants and demands such reflective assessment of its claim as it is possible for human reason to provide.

4. *Precisely as the task of an independent philosophy, philosophical theology is necessarily presupposed by a specifically Christian theology whose task is the fully reflective understanding of Christian faith.*

So formulated, this thesis applies to the special case of Christian theology certain general principles governing the relation between philosophy or philosophical theology and the reflective understanding of any particular religious faith. Such a formulation seems more than justified here because the motives behind this entire undertaking are those of a Christian theologian seeking fuller self-consciousness about his own specific task. Even so, it is important to recognize that the principles involved are not peculiarly Christian, but could be applied, *mutatis mutandis,* to any particular religion and theology whatever.

According to the view previously explained, religion in its various expressions is the primary and most direct reflection of the basic existential faith by which we all live simply as men. As such, it never exists in general, any more than art or science does, but always as a religion which has its origin in some particular occasion of insight or special revelation. Correlative with such revelation as the response through which it is received is a particular form of faith, which in turn provides the foundation for a whole structure of beliefs, rites, and social organizations. In many cases (although, admittedly, this is a variable which happens to be especially pronounced in Christianity), this religious structure is eventually subjected to reflective understanding, whereupon a theology of that religion appears on the scene. Naturally, since even the most direct and spontaneous religious expression is itself the product of understanding, it is already to some degree reflective and to that extent theology. But theology strictly so called is the more sustained, deliberate, and, therefore, specialized reflection whereby the primary expression of religion is subjected to critical analysis and interpretation.

As such, the theological understanding of a particular religion is obviously similar to what we have previously understood by "philosophy." In fact, we have ample warrant for asserting the following *analogia proportionalitatis:* Just as philosophy is the fully reflective understanding of our common faith simply as selves, so Christian theology, say, is the attempt to become fully self-conscious about specifically Christian faith. This assumes, of course, that Christianity is in the formal sense a religion just like any other. But, so far from being objectionable, this assumption clearly seems required both by the methods and conclusions of our best contemporary knowledge and by Christianity's own explicit statements about itself.

Having asserted this analogy, however, I would now call

attention to its peculiarity—a peculiarity that manifests itself in a number of ways, of which only the more important can be briefly considered.

In the first place, Christianity, being a religion, occupies what Whitehead speaks of as "the peculiar position" of religion, that it stands "between abstract metaphysics and the particular principles applying to only some among the experiences of life." [21] This being so, Christian theology cannot be regarded as merely one more special science and is not properly called a "science" at all unless it is in its own way absolutely basic and comprehensive. To be sure, it is unlike philosophy in that its origin is not simply in what I call "original revelation," meaning thereby the primal disclosure of reality as such as received somehow through our common faith as selves. Theology originates, rather, in a special revelation, which represents its relation to original revelation and to all other special revelations as that of *the* answer to a question. Thus the Johannine Christ is represented as saying, "Truly, truly, I say to you, before Abraham was, I am" (John 8:58). But, because of the peculiar nature of this answer, and so, of course, of the question it presupposes, Christian theology as the reflective understanding thereof cannot be less basic or comprehensive than philosophy itself. Hartshorne effectively confirms this when he observes that "religious ideas claim to be the concrete form of ultimate truths. . . . For religious ideas claim absolute ultimacy. They must involve all ultimate truths, which must be deducible from them. Otherwise, secular [namely, philosophical] truth would be more final than religious." [22] In this first important respect, then, Christian theology is not only like philosophy, but also has and must have the same ultimate basis and scope; for the revelation in which it has its origin is, by that revelation's own claim, the decisive re-presentation of God's original revelation to man as such, in which philosophy itself originates.

Christian theology is also like philosophy, indeed all reflection, in being essentially historical. Thus not only is it always a task performed in a particular cultural situation having definite possibilities and limitations, but it can hardly be accomplished save through critico-constructive discussion with the tradition of understanding in which the faith it would reflect has been previously reflected and re-presented. In the first instance, of course, this tradition is what is usually referred to as "the Christian tradition" in the broadest sense of the words, as comprising the beliefs, rites, social organizations, and theology of the Christian religion, as well as the rest of human life and culture so far as historically shaped thereby. As a matter of fact, Christian theology is essentially distinguished from philosophy in that the faith it seeks to understand is accessible even existentially, thanks only to its mediation by this quite particular tradition. But this is simply to say that theology's dependence on history reflects a still deeper dependence on it, which is based on the fact that the object of theological reflection is itself historically determined. Even so, theology's parallel with philosophy is close both because the "evidence" to which it attends comprises the whole of the Christian tradition and because it considers the properly theological element in this tradition always to have but secondary evidential force, relative to the more direct witness of the Christian community as contained primarily, though not exclusively, in Holy Scripture. Here again, however, the likeness between Christian theology and philosophy exhibits a peculiarity that makes it more than an ordinary analogy of proportionality. This is evident, first of all, in that theology's preunderstanding is one and the same with philosophy's. By the claim of Christian faith itself, whose witness is addressed to every man without exception, nothing is required by way of a preunderstanding of the Christian tradition beyond what is already required even for philosophical understanding, namely, the existential faith that constitutes human existence. Thus existential affirmation of the Christian faith is not a precondition of theological understanding, even though wherever such affirmation occurs the task of theology is set as an imperative task. But the peculiarity of the analogy also appears from the fact that the "evidence" to which theological reflection must attend cannot be restricted solely to the specifically Christian tradition, however broadly construed, or for all of its decisive importance. Just as religion in general is not merely coordinate with the other fields of culture, but is fundamental to, and uniquely representative of, them, so any religion claiming to be *the* religion can sustain its claim only if it is somehow expressed or implied by the whole of human life. In the last analysis, then, Christian theology not only is like philosophy in appealing to historical evidence, it appeals to the *same* evidence—even if in pursuit of its own distinctive task and thus with the aim of showing that such evidence both confirms and is confirmed by the specifically Christian faith it seeks to understand.

It would be possible to extend this comparative analysis by considering how theology is also like philosophy in having a constructive-synthetic as well as a critical-analytic function—or, as theologians would more likely put it, in being "systematic" (or "speculative") as well as "historical" (or "positive"). Likewise, we could consider how the task of theological understanding has come to be differentiated historically into several more special tasks, which nevertheless retain their essential unity insofar as they all contribute to the central responsibility of systematic theology. But extending the analysis in these ways could only confirm further what should already be sufficiently clear— that philosophy and Christian theology are not only closely analogous but because of the peculiar relation between their respective objects, between our basic existential faith and specifically Christian faith, also overlap or in a certain way coincide.

From this it follows that Christian theology necessarily presupposes philosophy, and that not simply in general or in any of philosophy's widely different forms, but in the quite particular form of philosophical theology or theistic metaphysics.

Because theology and philosophy by their very natures finally lay claim to the same basic ground, appeal to the same historical evidence—in short, serve an identical ultimate truth—their material conclusions must be in the last analysis mutually confirming, if either is to sustain its essential claim. This does not mean, of course, that their complete mutual confirmation must be actually realized, either now or at some time in the future. The essentially historical character of reflection, not to mention such other constants of the human equation as finitude and sin, hardly permits this as a real possibility. We simply have to reckon with the indefinite continuation of our present more or less irreducible pluralism of philosophical and theological positions. But, in doing so, we have no reason whatever to set aside the ideal that philosophy and theology alike establish as governing their relationship—even though we have the best of reasons for suspecting all claims to have already realized that ideal. So long as philosophy is a serious undertaking it involves the confidence, which it attempts to justify, that the truth of its material conclusions can only be confirmed by any true conclusions of Christian theology—and theology, naturally, involves and seeks to justify a corresponding confidence about the conclusions of philosophy.

Since our interest here is in theology's relation to philosophy, we must now consider more closely why the philosophy it presupposes must of necessity be a philosophical theology or a theistic metaphysics. The basic reason, of course, has already been given in pointing to the peculiar overlapping or coincidence of theological with philosophical understanding. But this reason can be developed in different ways, each of which is worth considering, even if it is implied by, as well as implies, the others.

One way begins with the observation that, for all the specificity of its origin and object, Christian theology is nevertheless an effort at reflective understanding, and so subject to the conditions of human reflection generally. Thus, for instance, it must seek to avoid the opposite evils of overcoming unclarity only at the price of incoherence and escaping inconsistency only by settling for vagueness. Or, it must satisfy the twin demands that its terms and assertions be logically consistent, both with themselves and with one another, and experientially significant, in that they are warranted somehow by our actual experience. But underlying all such conditions is the fact that theology is possible at all only in terms of concepts. "Reflective understanding" in the full sense applicable to theology means precisely conceptual understanding. Yet whence is theology to obtain its concepts, if not from philosophy? And what philosophy can provide the kind of conceptuality it needs except a complete theistic metaphysics?

The implied answers to these questions do not require us to suppose either that theology's dependence on philosophy is always direct or that individual theologians are necessarily dependent on other individuals who are philosophers. It is always possible, indeed likely, that the direct source of a theologian's principal concepts will be the specifically theological tradition in which he stands. Even so, if one investigates the provenance of these concepts, he is almost certain to discover the influence of some form of philosophical reflection directly proportional to the clarity and precision which recommend them for theological use. Similarly, it is perfectly possible that the philosophical reflection on which particular theologians are most dependent is precisely their own—that they are, as it were, their own philosophers. And yet, if such theologians are wise, they will be sensitive enough to the immense difficulties of their task to be eager for all the help they can get, and thus to maintain the most intensive and extensive discussion possible with their philosopher colleagues. By the same token, they will be particularly keen to learn everything they can from any philosophy that is sufficiently profound and comprehensive to clarify all the concepts necessary to an adequate reflective understanding of Christian faith.

Another way of making the same point proceeds from the fact that Christian theology is nothing if not the most serious possible concern with meaning and truth. This concern is so essential to theology not only because, being a form of reflective understanding, it could not fail to be thus concerned, but also, and crucially, because the faith it seeks to understand itself claims to be true and, therefore, to be meaningful as well. In making this claim, to be sure, Christian faith is no different from religion generally, at least the other world religions, which also make or imply the same kind of claim. But this should only make all the clearer why theology must be centrally concerned with vindicating the claim as it is advanced by Christian faith.

In this connection, it may be helpful to recall the familiar notion of "the risk of faith." This notion is usually taken to mean that, insofar as Christian faith is an understanding of one's existence to which there are in some sense real alternatives, it involves a choice, and so is in that respect a risk. Specifically, it is the risk that the basic truth of human existence is as it is represented to be in the witness of faith of Jesus Christ, or in the Christian special revelation. It follows, then, given the understanding of religion and theology previously developed, that there must be a reflective as well as an existential way of taking this risk, or, in other words, that the reflection of Christian faith in theological assertions is the venture of faith itself at the level of full self-consciousness. But to recognize this is to see once again why Christian theology is necessarily dependent not simply on some philosophy or other, but on an integral theistic metaphysics. For how can the venture of faith be reflectively confirmed, or theology's assertions rationally justified, except on the basis of just such a metaphysics?

To reply, as has often been done, that faith and theology do not need rational justification is either to ignore faith's own claim to be meaningful and true, or else to admit, in effect, that its claim is empty and not to be taken seriously. And this must be said as emphatically of current versions of the reply, which hold that "there can be no *general* justification of religion," [23] as of its more traditional versions, which maintain simply that faith is "above" reason and, therefore, cannot and need not be vindicated by it. There is no denying, of course, that philosophers do often exhibit "a craving for generality," and the reminder is insofar pertinent that "the distinction between the real and the unreal does not come to the same thing in every context." [24] But this in no way exempts theology from meeting the essential requirements of cognitive meaning. Hence, while it might be plausibly argued that Christian faith alone is a sufficient ground for the *truth* of theology's assertions, it would be plainly absurd to claim that it suffices to establish their *meaning*. Assertions as a rule can be established as meaningful, and hence as candidates for true belief, only by showing that they refer through at least some possible experience which could serve to verify them. Furthermore, in the case of theological assertions which in their logic are metaphysical, thus to establish their meaning is equivalent to establishing their truth; for either they can be shown to refer through *all* possible experience, or else they are doubtfully meaningful as metaphysical assertions. Thus not only is it evident that Christian faith alone is an insufficient ground for theology's assertions, but it is also clear that such assertions cannot even be established as meaningful except by establishing a theistic metaphysics which is true independently of specifically Christian faith.

Yet a third way of reaching the same conclusion develops the insight that the task of Christian theology is by its very nature hermeneutical. Up to this point, I have been at pains to avoid the term "hermeneutical" and its cognates because they have recently been so overused that they have tended to become a substitute for careful thinking, instead of being its instrument. But I have no reason to deny that the description of theology (and of philosophy too, for that matter) as a hermeneutical undertaking may be given an exact meaning by the account presented here. To the contrary, according to this account, theology is the reflective understanding of Christian faith, and thus, by direct implication, the critical interpretation of the witness of the Christian community.

But this conception of theology has some interesting implications that are not always recognized by proponents of "theology as hermeneutics." It implies, first of all, that theology must so interpret the witness of faith as to present faith itself as the decisive answer to the religious question of mankind. This implies, in turn, that the theologian must become fully self-conscious of the structure of this religious question, by understanding in an express, thematic, and conceptually precise way both the question itself and its "tacit presuppositions," including the criterion of the truth of any answer to it that these presuppositions contain. Yet, since the religious question can be nothing other than the existential question itself, thus to understand its logical structure, so as to interpret the Christian faith as the answer to it, is indistinguishable from working out a complete theistic metaphysics. Consequently, unless such a metaphysics were possible as the only adequate interpretation of our common faith, the task of Christian theology as a hermeneutical task could never be accomplished.

In all these ways, then, we see why the fully reflective understanding of the Christian faith necessarily presupposes an independent philosophical theology. And it should be just as evident that the independence of philosophical theology is crucial, since it is solely on this condition that Christian theology itself is possible and can accomplish its specific task. This does not mean, of course, that there is no sense at all in which philosophical theology, for its part, is also dependent on Christian reflection. Given the existence of the Christian religion and theology, they automatically become part, though only a part, of that "variety of expression" on which the philosopher by his calling is sworn to meditate. Moreover, we have seen that philosophy and Christian theology are in essence so related that they both serve the same ultimate truth, which implies that the philosopher's efforts to tell this truth are as responsible to the theologian as the theologian's are to him. Still, philosophy is and must be—for theology's sake as well as its own—independent of theology, in that it has its origin in human existence as such, rather than in human existence as historically determined by Christian faith. It is just insofar as philosophical theology preserves its independence as the full self-consciousness of our common faith as men that it both accomplishes its own essential task and also provides the indispensable presupposition of the specifically different task of Christian theology.

And just this specific difference is also at stake in the independence of philosophical theology. Only insofar as it is independent of Christian theology, as the general is of the special, or as the question is of the answer, is Christian theology itself clearly established as something different. Thus, contrary to what may have been inferred from this account, it has by no means collapsed the difference between theology and philosophy. In fact, I have stressed that theology is essentially distinguished from philosophy because the very object of its reflection is determined by a particular history, so that there would not even be any Christian theology save for specifically Christian revelation and faith. At the same time, I have indicated that it is Christian faith itself that sets the task of theological reflection as an imperative task of the Christian community. Because of its own inner nature and dynamic, faith seeks the fullest possible understanding of itself and its claim, and this means, finally, that it seeks a theological understanding. Hence the very faith that accounts for there being any Christian theology at all likewise accounts for theology's necessarily presupposing an independent philosophical theology. And yet the same faith also explains why theology can never be simply identified with philosophy, but abides in its specific difference as Christian faith itself on its way to full self-consciousness.

NOTES

1. According to Santayana, such faith is "the initial expression of animal vitality in the sphere of mind, the first announcement that anything is going on. It is involved in any pang of hunger, of fear, or of love. It launches the adventure of knowledge" (George Santayana, *Scepticism and Animal Faith: Introduction to a System of Philosophy* [Charles Scribner's Sons, 1923], pp. 180 f.).

2. See Arnold Gehlen, *Der Mensch, Seine Natur und seine Stellung in der Welt*, 8th ed. (Frankfurt: Athenaeum Verlag, 1966); also, Helmuth Plessner, *Die Stufen des Organischen und der Mensch*, 2d ed. (Berlin: Walter de Gruyter & Co., 1965).

3. Alfred North Whitehead, *The Function of Reason* (Princeton University Press, 1929), p. 10.

4. Lionel Rubinoff (ed.), *Faith and Reason: Essays in the Philosophy of Religion by R. G. Collingwood* (Quadrangle Books, Inc., 1968), pp. 108–121; also, pp. 122–147.

5. Cf. Ludwig Wittgenstein, *Philosophical Investigations*, 2d ed. (Oxford: Basil Blackwell & Mott, Ltd., 1958), p. 136 e: "Justification by experience comes to an end. If it did not it would not be justification."

6. Alfred North Whitehead, *Modes of Thought* (The Macmillan Company, 1938), p. 233.

7. *Ibid.*, pp. 96 f.; cf. Whitehead's *Adventures of Ideas* (The Macmillan Company, 1933), pp. 291 f.; and *Process and Reality: An Essay in Cosmology* (The Macmillan Company, 1929), pp. 317 f., where he states that "the best rendering" of "that ultimate, integral experience . . . whose elucidation is the final aim of philosophy" is "often to be found in the utterances of religious aspiration."

8. Whitehead, *Modes of Thought*, p. 17; cf. pp. 235 f.; also *Process and Reality*, p. 229, where "the metaphysical rule of evidence" is said to require that "we must bow to those presumptions which, in despite of criticism, we still employ for the regulation of our lives. Such presumptions are imperative in experience. Rationalism is the search for the coherence of such presumptions."

9. Whitehead, *Process and Reality*, p. 317.

10. John Passmore, *Philosophical Reasoning* (London: Gerald Duckworth & Co., Ltd., 1961), p. 78.

11. Whitehead, *Modes of Thought*, pp. 67, 237.

12. Cf. W. D. Hudson, *Ludwig Wittgenstein: The Bearing of His Philosophy Upon Religious Belief* (John Knox Press, 1968), pp. 61, 65.

13. Alfred North Whitehead, *Religion in the Making* (The Macmillan Company, 1926), p. 33.

14. Charles Hartshorne, *The Logic of Perfection and Other Essays in Neoclassical Metaphysics* (The Open Court Publishing Company, 1962), pp. 297, 131 f.

15. Charles Hartshorne, *Reality as Social Process: Studies in Metaphysics and Religion* (Free Press, 1953), p. 176; cf. *A Natural Theology for Our Time* (The Open Court Publishing Company, 1967), p. 32.

16. Whitehead, *Modes of Thought*, pp. 66, 69.

17. Charles Hartshorne, *Man's Vision of God and the Logic of Theism* (Harper & Brothers, 1941), p. 59.

18. Antony Flew, *God and Philosophy* (Harcourt, Brace and World, Inc., 1966), p. 28.

19. Cf. Emerich Coreth, *Metaphysik, Eine methodisch-systematische Grundlegung*, 2d ed. (Innsbruck: Tyrolia Verlag, 1964).

20. Flew, *op. cit.*, p. 124.

21. Whitehead, *Religion in the Making*, p. 31.

22. Hartshorne, *Man's Vision of God*, p. 113.

23. D. Z. Phillips, "Religious Belief and Philosophical Enquiry," *Theology*, Vol. LXXI, No. 573 (March, 1968), p. 120.

24. *Ibid.*, p. 115.

2

The Future of Philosophical Theology as Reflective Awareness

DAVID B. BURRELL

I wish to sketch out and to illustrate a role for rational discrimination in matters religious. The issue, I take it, is not *whether* we need critical reflection in these matters but rather *how* it should be engaged. In presenting a case for its appropriate exercise, I shall be exhibiting that quality of rational discrimination which seeks to understand where it is I stand—hence the term "reflective awareness." In doing so, I shall distinguish sharply between knowing *about* a language and knowing *how* to use a language, and allow this distinction to give body to an axiom that seems appropriate in matters religious: that one may only speak from where he is.

I shall assume that the most distinctive philosophical activity engages one in ferreting out criteria for responsible discoursing. I understand philosophy as a critical exercise, then, which eschews questing after that style of theoretic statement which could set reflective, critical awareness to rest. Yet in pursuing this activity, I have been forced to recognize multiple ambiguities in the working notion of criteria, particularly as they function in matters religious. Hence this paper has become an exercise in teasing out some pretensions in one's endeavor to formulate criteria for religious understanding—even while the paper engages us in that very endeavor. Like any philosophic exercise worthy of the name, it cannot take on basic questions without questioning itself.

1. THEOLOGICAL REFLECTION

The sources for theological reflection must inevitably be those activities which one describes as religious: the order of prayer represents the order of belief. However religious traditions may differ both in creed and in cult, there seem to be features that reappear. It is these features which tend to form the set of topics with which theology concerns itself: God, faith, grace or enlightenment, etc. These features tend to be those which reveal the shape of a religious tradition, and hence one may in fact speak of them without extensive acquaintance with the details of a tradition. They might well be called "formal features," for they not only reveal the contours of a particular tradition but also help to identify a way of life as religious. One need not prescribe them; they rather show themselves to be central to that activity which men recognize to be religious. Theology, then, does not represent a tradition over against the traditions which it studies, but is more like grammar with respect to working languages.[1] Grammar is not itself a competing language but rather a specialized type of reflection designed to show forth the structure of any particular language and so help one master his own language or acquire another.

So theology does not, for example, propose a picture of God for us, just as grammar does not take it upon itself to construct actual sentences. In this sense, theology is not charged with telling us what God is like, although a set of theological skills may well lead one to reject certain pictures actually proposed. In like manner, grammar does not discriminate among stories, although it may rule certain stories out as unintelligible. In this sense, theology as a reflective discipline reminds one of those "ideas of reason" which Kant discovered impossible to formulate yet unable to be dispensed with. The only solution is to become skilled in living with them.

To continue the suggestion of taking theology as grammar, a dispute among theologies is often like a grammatical dispute. The sense of what is being said may well be transmitted under either set of rules. It is not immediately evident, at any rate, that one style of theological reflection cancels out another way of bringing intelligibility to the same religious tradition. In this sense then, grammar comprises a set of rules organized to guide a know-how; it does not itself teach one *how to do* what is required. Yet we cannot forget that to fashion a grammar and to work with it in turn involves a certain know-how. One is reminded here of the therapist who can recognize a healthy person, even though it may prove extremely difficult for him to characterize such a person. And should he try to characterize "the healthy personality," he often finds himself listing relatively contradictory characteristics.[2] The resulting constellation of characteristics becomes a set of working criteria for psychic health. The criteria by which these characteristics were isolated, however, are simply not available. A reflective analysis may speak of overall norms such as "reconciling opposites," but these are clearly *post factum*. They do not function to select characteristics but are instead gleaned from the characteristics collated by the experienced therapist.

1.1. The Transcendence-Criterion: "Infinite Qualitative Difference"

In a similar fashion to the psychologist's invoking so generic a criterion for mental health as "reconciliation of opposites," so theologians are fond of demanding that language about God respect the "infinite qualitative difference" between God and creatures. Yet if we look closely at how they in fact formulate this recommendation into functioning criteria, we will notice a set of logical concerns delicately guided by one's religious experience. The most lucid example available to me is Aquinas' establishing that God is *simple*.[3] If we look closely at the question in the *Summa* which establishes the conditions for whatever may be attributed to God, we notice that Aquinas is formulating not descriptive characteristics so much as syntactical rules for regulating well-formed statements about God. That is to say, his affirming that God is *simple* is not meant to exclude his being complicated, but rather to exclude saying anything of him at all after the fashion in which we speak about an object *in* the universe.

What Question 3 on God's *simplicity* actually does is to remind us of the consequences for discourse about God which follow upon accepting him as the source and origin of all things.[4] Aquinas means by these constraints to interdict any discourse about God which proves *objectifying*. Hence, God cannot properly be conceived as a physical object (3.1), nor described in a proposition designed to articulate form and matter (3.2), nor spoken about in such a way as to locate him within a kind (3.5), nor in any other way described as we are wont to describe the objects of our experience (3.6–7). What, then, can be said about God? Literally *nothing*, if we understand that in speaking *about* something we are inescapably attributing something of something else. This proves to be Aquinas' way of showing that in the most basic logical space of all—the proposition articulated into subject and predicate—God cannot be accommodated.[5] Yet Aquinas would be the last to claim that these austere restrictions result from an esoteric mystical insight. They are simply the logical consequences of defining God as source and origin of all things, for then he could not logically be one of those things, and the only way in which we can display that fact is to insist that he be so utterly different as to elude that form shared by proposition and fact: subject/predicate or matter/form.

If anything can be said of God, it *cannot* be said in a manner in which it is said of x that x F's. If we want to say, for example, that God is just, then we must show in the manner in which we use this expression that we are equally entitled to assert that God is justice.[6] Whatever can be said, then, can only properly be said when it expresses this syntactic "fact" that an ordinary sentence will distort the message. A proper expression will succeed in *showing* its own inadequacy. Hence religious expressions are properly formed to the extent that they manifest their own inadequacy in their effort to address or to remark upon God. Although Aquinas himself did not speak in so expressly metalinguistic a fashion, to translate his statements succeeds in reconciling his explicitly negative strictures on theological discourse with his speaking as a theologian.[7]

This manner of laying out Aquinas' theological criteria also sheds unexpected light upon the recurring question about statements including the term "God": do they intend to state something about God or about the relation between the speaker and God?[8] An appropriate answer would be: neither and both. That is, such statements succeed in *stating* that God is such and such to the extent that they also *express* a relation between the speaker and God which contributes the awareness that God's being such and such *is* God himself. Graphically, this consciousness on the part of the speaker is manifested by the manner in which he goes on to use whatever statements he may have made about God. By disallowing certain implications, for example, or by clearly showing that in attributing something of God he is accepting that statement as norm for all others, he succeeds in showing that he comprehends the rules for appropriate and well-formed statements about God.

This brief sketch of Aquinas' foundations for a theological reflection on religious language serves as a useful introduction to the position that I shall defend. It also gives sufficient attention to the tradition out of which I speak and shows the extent to which I feel free in putting it to a use which is conceptually quite novel. (I should want to feel that there is a radical continuity of intent between Aquinas and myself, but that is one of those peculiarly Catholic concerns.) The position which I shall sketch out is beholden to the tools of contemporary linguistics and logical analysis as well as to the theological acumen of giants like Aquinas. The questions which I shall attend to are those raised more recently by descriptive/nondescriptive considerations, demands for nonobjectifying discourse, and most generally by recent reflections on the role philosophy has to play in helping us get clear about the manner in which we speak of and speak to God. I shall confess to a predilection for Wittgenstein, and shall try to show why and how it is that we seem to be able to develop a critical capacity for telling whether a preacher has anything to say, and for delineating those features of our contemporary scene which might be authentically religious. In the process, I hope to show something of the utility as well as the superfluity of theology. To signal my gratitude to Wittgenstein, I wish to examine more closely at this time his metaphor of theology as grammar.

1.2. Examining the Grammar Metaphor

Here and elsewhere in Wittgenstein's writings, "grammar" is used in a shifting sense: roughly as that skill which allows one to call attention to the shape of what is said, and from that shape alone remark about the propriety of what has been said. To speak of a grammatical investigation is to focus our attention on the manner in which something is being said, and hence to teach us to attend to what a statement shows in saying what it says.

Yet the discipline of grammar as such only envisions well-formed sentences. By extension, we may call "grammatical" that discipline which adjudges works from their structural characteristics. In this sense, literary criticism can be considered such a discipline, and the literary critic one who teaches us how to assess a work by learning to pay special attention to the manner in which it is formed. (I shall not feel obliged to distinguish between *syntax* and *semantics* in this discussion of grammatical considerations. In fact, after Wittgenstein's careful attention to the ways in which we use expressions, that earlier distinction becomes less and less useful. It could certainly be argued that only one who can recognize good writing can qualify as a grammarian. Semantics precedes syntax, even though one's subsequent concern with formal or structural criticism may sound suspiciously detached from that multitude of skills which make for good reading and good writing.) Sometimes, though not always, the skills developed in criticizing help one to compose—to tell a story or to paint a picture. One thinks here especially of Tolkien, a linguist who first worked out a language from different Middle English sources and then constructed the Middle Earth in which his language is spoken.

I have employed the grammar metaphor from Wittgenstein principally to remind us of that sort of discipline which develops critical attention to form. We moved quickly from professional grammarian to literary critic. This allows me to introduce an initial clarifying comparison for the theologian: he plays much the same role toward elucidation of ritual and religious myth as the literary critic does toward a work of art, literary or dramatic. The task is one of assessment: what is it about this work which insinuates me more profoundly and congruently into my own existence, or what is it about the work which blocks such a process? The literary critic is a useful example because he rarely claims to be in possession of a set of criteria from whence he judges—unless of course he be an ideological critic who simply measures the work through a theory of behavior.[9] The work itself is allowed to do its job, and the task of criticism itself involves judgments which can be rubrically characterized—coherence, unity, sensibility—but never successfully formulated. That is, there is no general science of criticism or of interpretation. The best a critic can do is to judge how appropriate the language is to the task which the author sets himself. Nor can that task be stated independently; one's conception of it must arise from a sensitive reading and going along with the work itself.

2. Roles of a Theologian

It does not seem, then, that a theologian is commissioned to tell a new story or to tell it better than it has been told—if by that we mean to replace the original story. Nor would he be called to *explain* revelation with a yet more comprehensive scheme. The paradigm of *explanation* demands that the scheme offered tell why what in fact occurs does occur, either by showing forth the intimate structural characteristics of what occurs or by revealing the intentions of the one who plans it.[10] On the model which I have illustrated from Aquinas and adopted as my own, the task of a theologian is rather to develop (in himself and in others) the skills necessary to recognize the decisive notions which give a specific shape to a religious tradition. This developed capacity to recognize formal features of discourse will assist him as he attempts to formulate these features more perspicuously as a set of rules for well-formed religious utterances.

In fact, he will be called upon to discriminate among those many inevitable efforts to retell the story, and to discriminate among them on grounds analogous to those employed by a literary critic. This role might be termed *critical* or *analytic*. In doing so, the theologian will be able to count upon those skills which he has developed in coming to grips with the primary documents of his own religious tradition. Finally, he may undertake deliberately to retell the story or (perhaps more authentically) to exercise his imaginative powers in helping others to recognize the lineaments of the original story in unfamiliar settings. In this fashion, the power of the story to illuminate one's life is substantially enhanced. (This last description is that theological role expressedly undertaken by Tillich and termed "the method of correlation"; it may be termed *constructive*.)

Before illustrating how these internally related roles may

function, I should meet the logical question: What criteria does the theologian employ in his work? My preliminary response will be that these criteria are displayed and cannot be articulated. The reasons for this response will become clearer as the discussion proceeds. Formulated generally, they amount to reminding us that "criteria" are functioning in an extended or analogous way here. That is, we presume that the endeavor is rule-bound if it merits the name of "discipline." But like "semantic rules," criteria for assessing and judging are notoriously elusive.[11] Furthermore, these criteria are displayed not only in the actual theological reflection carried out but even more significantly in the quality of religious life countenanced and encouraged by those rules of formation which delineate the form of a particular religious tradition.

In this sense, the doing of theology cannot be represented as a "higher level" of endeavor than that of living a religious life. It simply represents a different perspective on the religious journey—specifically a *formal* perspective. To assume this perspective skillfully is to know how to stem the demand for criteria raised now with respect to one's theological reflection, for the question of appropriate norms for discourse can always be re-iterated, unless one has succeeded in showing that his critical procedure is a perspicuously logical one.[12] This may well be an impossible goal, but it does provide the aim for laying out the formal structures of religious discourse: to exhibit how one goes about the business of critical assessment. If this is the business of theology, engaging in it will ready someone to do it himself.

Although the particular schemes employed by a theological critic remain dispensable, the skills acquired prove invaluable. Nor can we overlook the fact that theological reflection will normally be in order precisely to help release one from the grips of another interpretive scheme originally adduced to clarify. Theology is dispensable, then, in the same measure that therapy is. A healthy person need not succumb to insinuations that he must undergo explicit therapy, yet if he reflects upon those factors which have contributed to his present posture, he will discover many relationships whose dynamics have proven therapeutic.

By taking up the expressive comparison of theology to grammar and even more amply to literary criticism, I am not relying on dreams of "universal grammar" to suggest a generic critical method. There will be as many theologies as there are critical postures, although certain extremely general statements would seem to guide any constructive or critical endeavor. Hence, for example, one cannot help inquiring after the unity and coherence of a work. So certain statements govern any religious expression. I have alluded to the controlling criterion of "infinite qualitative difference." A useful exercise in developing theological skills is to notice how and in what varied ways this exigency emerged as a criterion in the discussions surrounding *homo-ousion* as contrasted with *homoi-ousion* at Nicaea.[13]

If the statements about or addressed to God must be constructed so as to display my ignorance, then the language must be employed in such a way as to intimately involve me. That is, the expressions involved must be of a sort which allow the speaker to grow into them, as it were; and the extent to which he has grown into them will be manifest in the manner in which he uses them.[14] (I have argued elsewhere that the tradition which invoked analogous terms and went on to construct a "doctrine of analogy" comes to this: a privileged set of expressions without any determinate meaning and thus capable of unusual plasticity, together with a speaker who knows how to use them.[15]) A language into which I might grow, as it were, must be one capable of expressing not only where I am but what I aspire to become. For then and only then will the language be able to *say* one thing and *show* that this way of putting it falls short of my intent. That is, the expressions involved will be of a sort which announce that one can never pretend to use them "properly"—or to put it another way, the expressions will show that their proper use always outreaches the particular conception we have adapted for the present. The Socratic formula, the wise man is one who realizes that he is not wise, becomes a rule for distinguishing those expressions capable of being put to such self-conscious use. It is not necessary that everyone who uses them be aware that this particular use falls short of the reach of the expression, for the syntax of the expression is such that a Socrates can always show him how the constricted way in which he may be using the expression does not exploit its full potentiality.

When I speak of language, then, I am not referring simply to a set of expressions, but principally to the "fact" that I am forced to adopt certain ways of speaking. Furthermore, some of the reasons why I am forced to adopt them can show themselves in the manner in which I use the expressions that I do. It is "facts" like these that a search for criteria of proper religious discourse turns up. Hence the study is not merely one of language as a set of expressions but more significantly of the speaker as one who is employing a particular language to a conscious end. The fact that he selects the expressions which he does, together with the manner in which he employs them, both serve to reflect something of the shape of that about which he is discoursing or to which he is speaking.

This is the best expression I can muster for bringing the norms governing these reflections of mine up for scrutiny. I mean furthermore consciously to call attention to my indebtedness to the *Tractatus* in putting it as I have, for if Wittgenstein discovered his dreams of a logical form to have been naïve, he never relinquished his assurance that the expressions which I am constrained to adopt, together with the manner in which I construct them, show forth the essential properties of the subject matter in question. "The fact that the propositions of logic are tautologies shows the formal-logical properties of language and the world"; the fact that I have recourse to expressions of analogous logical form, together with the manner in which I put them together in an effort to say what I wish to say, shows something of the contour of that universe of discourse called divine.[16] It is this central methodological and metaphysical thesis which signals my indebtedness to Wittgenstein.

3. How Theological Criticism Operates

One has a right to ask at this point how a theologian might undertake the sort of critical exercise that I have recommended. In fact, there is no other way to give my recommendations a definite sense without showing what I mean by an actual example.[17] I have remarked that Aquinas provided us with some grammatical hints concerning the construction of particular statements, notably in his article on the "simplicity" of God but also developed in Questions 3 through 13 of the first part of the Summa theologiae. However, besides grammatical rules for the formation of individual statements, there are also critical recommendations to guide correct composition. These are less amenable to precise formulation than grammatical remarks, but they reflect how the metaphor of theologian as grammarian quickly opens out into the broader one of theologian as literary critic.

3.1. Some General Considerations

I should insist above all on painstaking effort at accuracy of expression. This means eschewing or exploding clichés, especially theological ones. It also involves using the images which we will inevitably employ both with finesse and when necessary with a commentary directing us how we are to understand them. (The New Testament descriptions of Jesus' leaving his apostles for the last time provide exemplars for this form of expression. The very construction of the Marcan text makes it clear that Jesus' departure amounts to his active presence [Mark 16:19], whereas Luke put this same understanding in the provocative words of the angel: "Why are you standing here looking up into the sky?" [Acts 1:11].)

I prefer these general recommendations to a complete list, if only to show that following even these few will guarantee sharpening one's sense for discriminating the authentic from the inauthentic voice in preaching, praying, or discoursing about these matters. The attention to language that I have recommended shapes a process whereby one cannot help becoming increasingly aware of what he is up to in using the expressions that he finds himself using in the manner in which he does use them. Aspiring to clarity in these matters accustoms us to the ignorance and unknowing which plagues us here, while a deliberately destructive campaign against theological clichés gives vent to our aspirations for unity of mind and heart in this arena of discourse. The ideal aspired to is that one speak only and completely from where he is; that the statements he employs express his relationship to God by exhibiting a poignant awareness that *what* is said *will* prove misleading to the extent that it relies on accepted grammatical form.

But this represents a despairingly exigent ideal! Precisely how is the theologian to measure such awareness? What are the bench marks for showing the inadequacy of an expression? How is it that the manner in which the expressions are employed can manage to exhibit an appropriate measure of self-awareness? The fact that we can raise these questions suggests that all my discussion of language and its appropriate use simply postpones the nagging metaphysical issues. Like Rudolf Carnap's division of language into *formal* and *material* modes, all the interesting questions crop up again[18]—questions such as: Why must we employ the expressions Aquinas singles out? What are the criteria by which we discriminate authentic from inauthentic religious talk? How can we ascertain that requisite awareness of inappropriateness which (curiously enough) makes for appropriateness in matters religious, by simply looking at the words on the page or hearing them spoken?

Before meeting these objections in the manner in which they can be met, it is useful to note that I regard them more as reassurances than as objections, for their occurrence would be crippling only if I were to pretend that a systematically linguistic turn introduces us into a completely new problematic. Rather, I find it reassuring to note the continuity between philosophic theology as I conceive it and natural theology of the past. Similar questions remain to be answered after one executes a linguistic turn. Chances are we shall still have competing critical procedures as in the past we have had competing theological systems. Just as literary critics divide according to the predilections they display for different criteria of criticism, so theological criticism will inevitably divide according to how one purports to distinguish authentic from inauthentic religious discourse. What is new in the approach which I have recommended and shall defend is better illustrated than said, and will be illustrated in reviewing a theological commentary on *emptiness* in Buddhist religious speech.

3.2. ISSUES OF MEANING AND JUSTIFICATION: METAPHYSICS

One might also wonder whether this approach sheds any further light on the vexing question whether theological statements are *about* God or man? I have expressly required a rigorous translation into a special set of terms, yet insist that even these prove ever inadequate to speak of God. Why use only these terms? And how do we know even then that we are speaking about God and not simply referring to human aspirations? The response to the second question, I shall contend, is contained in the response to the first. The so-called "problem of reference" is not a distinct one from that of meaning. Rather, it seems to be the case that the principal guarantee of accurate reference is definiteness of sense. And the requirements for definiteness of sense as elaborated in theological criticism we shall illustrate in reviewing Buddhist expressions for emptiness.

What is genuinely new and in fact revolutionary about this approach is the conception of metaphysics which it implies. Or perhaps it would be better to speak of a new clarity about what it is to *do* metaphysics. The issue may be joined in the following terms: May we speak of the most basic level of philosophical reflection as though it were a theory among theories, albeit the most general theory, and engage in it as though we could lay it out in a more or less coherent set of statements which would thereby create a matrix legitimizing yet other statements? Or is that most basic level of reflective human self-awareness (which some are wont to call metaphysics) another sort of thing altogether?

Were it another sort of thing altogether, we should only know that it was if it were able to show itself to be utterly different. It could do so, paradoxically enough, by being *unable* to formulate its primary principles or to come clean on the criteria which it employs and in terms of which it assesses. In fact, that form of philosophic reflection which was "most basic" would certainly have to be in such a fix. It would differ furthermore from mere unreflective theorizing, in being aware of the fix in which it is and endeavoring to *show* that awareness in the way in which it proceeds. Of course, one may simply *think* he has reached that level of reflection which is "most basic"; presumably the role of logical and philosophical expertise is to show up pseudolimits as less than basic.

Should this style of reflection recommend itself to us, it would have to do so on entirely other grounds than those of *justification*, because there would exist no terms in which it could be justified. It must, rather, recommend itself to a discriminating person by serving as a way whereby one can become an even more discriminating person. In this sense, we could speak loosely of this most basic level of philosophical reflection as the most general theory of all, because we would then appreciate that the word "theory" was being used in a misleading way. For we should by then appreciate that there is no apparatus

in the methods appropriate to theory construction to show someone that his theory qualifies as "the most general," whereas
philosophical reflection is precisely that manner of coming to
grips with one's own presuppositions which could recognize a
limit of discourse to be a limit of discourse—if anything could.

Just as critical reflection does employ schemes, however, so
this way of doing metaphysics will entail some construction and
theory-building. But the task itself is more properly a discipline
than a set of statements, more accurately embodied as a skill
than stated as a set of postulates. I shall want to make the strong
claim, furthermore, that what is new in this conception of doing
metaphysics captures what is authentic in the best of classical
philosophizing. I can defend this claim most economically if
one grants that the genius of Plato and Aristotle in effecting a
transition from *mythos* to *logos* was their attention to form.
When one is directed from the many responses to the question,
What is it? to consider the question itself as a question form, he
undertakes an entirely new kind of thinking that I have called
"reflection." This manner of thinking yields *categories*, that is,
generalizations about the manner in which something is said to
be the case. The quest for categories allows one to anatomize
what can be said by laying down rules for saying it correctly, and
rules as well for saying other things once these things have been
said. This process can be improved upon and new languages
invented for special reasons, but the single-minded intent is to
lay language out in such a way as to display the true joints of the
world.

What cannot be said, however, and hence cannot be anato-
mized in this fashion is precisely that attention to the form of
our discourse which effected this very transition to critical reflection. And since it cannot be laid out, there is a tendency to
overlook its distinctive quality. Hence the transition from
straightforward statement to critical reflection is never something
accomplished once for all, but something which each thinker
needs to effect in his own thinking and life of thought. (This,

I take it, is what Heidegger speaks of when he speaks of recovering being.[19]) The reflective capacity elicited by directing our attention to the form of what is said develops capabilities of laying hold of what one is doing so that he can understand it and accomplish it more single-mindedly.

Roughly speaking, then, the alternatives are to consider that most basic level of philosophic discourse called "metaphysics" either as saying something about everything or as an attempt to lay hold of what one is doing in speaking as he does. The first conception requires a special language such as "being and its modes" to show that it is speaking about everything, whereas the second program demands exercise in using what language we have in such a way as to call attention to the manner in which we are using it. The aim of the first program is to speak directly about the world as a transempirical (and hence metaphysical) object; the aim of the second program is more simply to speak responsibly. Yet for all its modesty, it is no less pretentious in seeking to lay out the joints of the world. For to speak responsibly means to tell it like it is insofar as one can perceive it for what it is. In this sense, the second conception of doing metaphysics would seem to address itself to all of the issues grappled with by traditional philosophical reflection, and do so in a manner free from the more objectionable pretentions of metaphysics as a most general theory about transempirical objects.

What this program has to offer is a method for rejecting that characterization of metaphysics without thereby junking the precious philosophical reflections of the ancients about the limits of our discourse and the form of our speaking about the world.

3.3. "EMPTINESS"—A STUDY IN RELIGIOUS MEANING

Frederick Streng has given us a study of Nagarjuna's second-century exercise in religious understanding as it focuses on *sunyata.*[20] His investigation of Nagarjuna's use of the term "emptiness" will prove an apt illustration of theology as criticism and also provide the opportunity for making observations beyond those which Streng himself makes. By an unrelenting logical analysis strikingly similar in tenor and outlook to that pursued by W. V. O. Quine, Nagarjuna discovers that we are at a loss to know whether words do in fact refer to the things which they pretend to name. What Nagarjuna has discovered and proceeds to demonstrate to us is what Quine would call the "inscrutability of reference." [21] Nagarjuna assumes that one's rudimentary analysis of the power of language to express what is the case will fasten upon the manner in which words purport to name things. He then proceeds to show, by a relentless accumulation of destructive logical exercises, that a language understood in this manner cannot express anything. One can only conclude, if he retains the initial picture, that nothing exists: "All is empty."

Yet Nagarjuna succeeds in bringing his protagonist to this point only in the measure that he can understand the author's careful logical analysis. So if the result of Nagarjuna's demanding dialectic is destructive, nevertheless the very process whereby the author succeeds in showing how vain it is to imagine that words refer to things remains a quite positive achievement. Since both author and reader can claim to be in possession of at least this discipline, *that* realization amounts to enlightenment.

Like Camus' early and relentless analysis of the human situation in *The Myth of Sisyphus*, this exercise yields no "positive" results. Yet unlike Camus, Nagarjuna does not presume to evaluate its results. Who can say that the fact that "all is empty" is absurd? Rather, Nagarjuna recalls us to the discipline itself and succeeds in showing forth the limits of understanding by continuing to show us that we cannot have what we seem to be striving for yet which logic prohibits us from coveting: namely, a commensurate grasp of what is really the case. He does not presume to evaluate the results for the meaning of one's life; quite the contrary, the thrust of Buddhist religious rhetoric concerns itself with showing how life can indeed have meaning in the face of apparent emptiness. Nagarjuna shows affinities with Camus in valuing consciousness above all else, but displays greater maturity in hesitating to tie down the initially negative connotations of "emptiness" by invoking "the absurd." [22]

In the case of Nagarjuna, it is a matter of denying that, on a name/thing reference theory of language, we can manage to speak right out *what is*. What he does show is the instability of such an epistemological posture and its incoherence as a semantic theory. He is not inclined to a reflective turn at this point, however, but tends rather to accept the theory and move to a radical religious posture. In terms that I shall want to employ, he feels that he has run afoul of the limits of discourse, and recognizing a limit for what it is, rigorously eschews any attempt to lay hold of it. He instead respects the logic of limits and spends his energy and talent bumping against this limit in ways designed to reveal its contours. [23]

In this sense, Nagarjuna reminds us of Hume, and was destined to enjoy his currency. For it *does* seem that the name/thing reference theory of language captures a commonsense semantics, so that Nagarjuna succeeds in formulating what in fact is the limit for most. This direction of attention explains the initially implausible claim that Buddhism is empiricist and it also reminds us of Quine's observation that one who is scandalized by the inscrutability of reference can only be so because he has presumed that there was in fact "something to scrute." [24] Without such a presupposition, Nagarjuna's conclusions are not quite so radical as he thought, for he may not have succeeded in reaching the limit of discourse, yet the lesson of his logical exercise remains instructive.

3.4. WHAT THE EXAMPLE SHOWS

In my case I have been trying to show that any attempt to come forward with a most general theory will prove semantically incoherent. The reason is simple but elusive: the very model employed—that of a general theory—does not contain sufficient reflective acumen about establishing its generality. And I can assert this precisely because it presents itself as a most general theory. For the categories in which the theory itself is cast must then provide the limits of discourse, but to work with them and formulate them as a theory demands a capacity for working with the limits of discourse which belies their being limits.[25]

The purpose of my critique, like Nagarjuna's, is to expose a current paradigm and show its ineptitude for achieving what it must pretend to achieve: a more adequate understanding of God. Unlike Nagarjuna, I shall not, however, presume that we have reached the bounds of sense, but simply have shown that an apparent limit is not a limit in fact. The fact that we thought it to be the limit of our understanding betrays how confined a set of canons of understanding we had been employing.

So where Nagarjuna had no moves left, and could only say no and introduce sunyata, the manner in which our critique has been proceeding leaves much more room to move. All that is demanded is that my proposal not be presented in the spirit of an alternative theory, for one can no longer move in the direction whose pretensions we have exposed.

Rather, one may try to give voice to other ways of understanding than those captured by explanation. Wittgenstein, for example, often spoke of his statements in the *Tractatus* as having an ability to elucidate the logical features of our situation.[26] It will not suffice, of course, simply to adopt another term. We must show that the mode and style of reflection which issues in elucidating the logical features of a situation involves quite different sorts of procedures than do explanations proceeding by way of general theory.

Yet there is a question to which one may appear vulnerable. Where do I stand? Have I not a position? If so, what makes it better than another position? Must I not formulate my position to lay it open to criticism of the kind that I have submitted others to? In short, does not the very direction of my criticism imply that I too have a "doctrine of God"? And if this is the case, have we not come full circle to a quite traditional conception of theologizing?

Because the expression is inescapably vague and the metaphor all-pervasive, one cannot easily deny "having a position," yet one can eschew formulating it in such a way as to pretend to be in possession of a yet more general theory about the world. Rather, one may remark as we have about what it means to trust that intelligence which has allowed us to see what Nagarjuna is doing as well as what we are doing. Philosophy, then, becomes more a path to enlightenment than an attempt at explanation, and proceeds more by therapy than by constructive efforts. I have used Streng's analysis of Nagarjuna to show that sunyata, or "emptiness," functions as it does in an effort to offset and to correct a naïve theory of meaning. To use his analysis in this way is to call our attention to the fact that we possess and use many expressions which do not refer, and that those which do refer do so only in the measure in which we can establish their sense. How do we know all this? By proceeding and succeeding in showing the force of the distinction between *sense* and *reference* in the manner in which language functions. Yet to appreciate this fact about our language does not demand that we invent a new one—that we reconstruct reality by proposing a logic appropriate to the deeper level to which our appreciation has carried us.

4. SUMMARY: BEYOND SYSTEM
TO ENLIGHTENMENT THROUGH THERAPY

The aim of all that we have been doing up to now has been to bring ourselves to the point of recognizing schemes for what they are. The way in which we come to recognize them is by calling attention to the manner in which we employ them to do different jobs, and the capacity we have to find them adequate to the task or not. Understanding, then, how we use conceptual frameworks as handles to lay hold of the subject matter in question, we should be sufficiently free from any urge to construct a new one to rely upon.[27] For it is enough certainly to rely upon the skills which have brought us to this point. When philosophy becomes a way of enlightenment in this fashion by employing discourse in a therapeutic way, we can gradually free ourselves from a foundational model for human understanding.[28] Relying upon the critical skills that shape the doing of philosophy does not amount to taking up a new position, though the sustained exercise of these skills may well show up certain "positions" or inference schemes to be inappropriate.

But what of the traditional way of conceiving philosophy's role vis-à-vis theology: to provide a language so that one can speak of God adequately enough to respond to the invitation offered in revelation? Once again, this role may be conceived as passé or reinterpreted in a paradoxical manner. I should say that what we have called "the infinite qualitative difference" prohibits philosophy from pretending to provide a language *tout court.*[29] Yet what philosophical reflection can do has been illustrated after our manner of taking Aquinas. In contemporary terms, a skilled dialectician approaching the realm of theological discourse should be able to show in what form the question is posed for a religious response: it must be such that *nothing* can pretend to answer it. (This is a semantic rendering of Jesus' words: "Without me you can do nothing" [John 15:5].)

I may illustrate this central point of the essay by reference to Kierkegaard's use of "the Unknown." In the *Fragments,* Kierkegaard makes his point by naming the limits which a passionate Reason seeks to embrace "the Unknown." I have found it useful to parse this name by the question-form: Is it all worth it, or does it all make sense? The "answer" to such an utterly basic question would be something like "the Truth"—that is, the *secret* which animates everything else I do. In these terms, the formula that Aquinas employed to carry the meaning of

"God"—"source and origin of all things"—becomes less a cosmological notion and instead more like "the point of it all." Furthermore, if we paraphrase the Hegelian expression "the Unknown" as a question-form, it becomes apparent that Kierkegaard is using Hegelian shorthand to make a point.

We have only to ask ourselves, What possibly could *show* that it was all worth it or that it makes sense? What could count as showing that it all makes sense? Socratically, all that one can say is that he must have faith in reason or all is lost. Beyond that he cannot go. In other terms, should anyone want him to affirm that being is intelligible, he would not know how to do it.[30] Christianly we are told that it all does make sense, since God is our Father. But we are not told *how* it makes sense. The God who is dead is the one who purported to explain how it is all worthwhile. But in order that he might serve as an explanation, it was necessary to formulate him in terms that we could understand. The result, of course, was that he ceased to be God. Furthermore, when it became apparent that he did not succeed in explaining either, he slipped quietly from the scene.

To come to this point, to appreciate this fact, is to signal the end of philosophy as an attempt to explain in systematic terms that it all makes sense. To recognize the futility—indeed the comic quality—of trying to show *how* it all makes sense is to begin to live philosophically. Hence the closest thing to an affirmation that being is in fact intelligible which we possess lies in our recognizing that nothing could possibly show us that fact. To paraphrase Nagarjuna: on an explanatory paradigm, God is nothingness.

And once we have seen that the questions which shape religious responses are properly speaking unanswerable, we are prepared to be astonished at the manner in which revelation addresses itself to these questions. What one finds increasingly remarkable in the Gospel is the manner in which religious questions are transformed from within. Hence if anything could count as "an answer," these story accounts would do so. But they fill the purpose that they do precisely by renouncing that role. What is this except to note in yet other terms the "infinitive qualitative difference": the God who reveals himself in Jesus cannot be simply equated with the "meaning of my life"? If he is to be the Truth, in the sense of the secret which animates my life, then he is so only to the extent that he is also the Way which leads me to appreciate that nothing can answer my questions in an explanatory manner, and that the Life into which I am ushered is something beyond my wildest dreams or expectations.

The discipline that doing philosophy accomplishes readies one to hear language of this sort, and equips him with skills enough to assess its meaning and its power. What no discipline can do, however, is to dispense one from undertaking the journey which this language invites and demands. Quite the contrary, in the precise measure in which one comes to acquire the discipline which is philosophy by having undertaken it, he will realize that any promise of critical understanding which dispenses one from engaging in the appropriate discipline remains an empty promise because it offers content without its requisite form.

NOTES

1. The clue comes from Wittgenstein: "Grammar tells what kind of object anything is. (Theology as grammar.)" (*Philosophical Investigations* [The Macmillan Company, 1963], p. 373).

2. Abraham Maslow gives a revealing list of characteristics of the "healthy person" in *Psychology of Being*, 2d ed. (D. Van Nostrand Company, Inc., 1969), p. 26: "(1) Superior perception of reality, (2) increased acceptance of self, of others and of nature, (3) increased spontaneity, (4) increase in problem-centering, (5) increased detachment and desire for privacy, (6) increased autonomy and resistance to enculturation, (7) greater freshness of appreciation and richness of emotional reaction, (8) higher frequency of peak experiences, (9) increased identification with the human species, (10) changed (the clinician would say, improved) interpersonal relations, (11) more democratic character struc-

ture, (12) greatly increased creativeness, (13) certain changes in the value system."

3. *Summa theologiae* I, 3, in Timothy McDermott (ed.), *Existence and Nature of God*, Vol. II of *Summa theologiae* (McGraw-Hill Book Company, Inc., 1964).

4. Following Preller (cf. Note 7), I have found it not only possible but profitable to bracket any existential implications of Question 2, and simply regard those exercises as ways of establishing the propriety of speaking of a "source and origin of all things." Having introduced us to language of that sort, Question 3 and subsequent questions can hinge arguments on the assertion that God is the primary existent (*Deus est primum ens*, 3.1., 3.8), where again we are speaking of the consequences which must follow upon so understanding "God."

5. In the material mode that Aquinas normally employs: "It is plain that God does not belong to the genus of substance" (3.5.1.), which is to say that "nothing is commensurate with God" (3.5.2.).

6. This is the gist of Aquinas' explicit recourse to the "formal mode" in 3.3.1: "In talking about simple things we have to use as models the composite things from which our knowledge derives. Thus when God is being referred to as a subsistent thing, we use concrete nouns (since the subsistent things with which we are familiar are composite); but to express God's simpleness we use abstract nouns. So that when we talk of godhead or life or something of that sort residing in God, the diversity this implies is not to be attributed to God himself, but to the way in which we conceive him."

7. Cf. Victor Preller, *Divine Science and the Science of God* (Princeton University Press, 1967), and my review of this analytically careful and philosophically strategic book "Religious Life and Understanding," in *Review of Metaphysics*, Vol. 22 (1969), pp. 681–690.

8. This issue forms the focus of Aquinas, *Summa theologiae* I, 13, especially 13.2, 13.3, 13.4, and 13.12, in Herbert McCabe (ed.), *Knowing and Naming God*, Vol. III of *Summa theologiae* (McGraw-Hill Book Company, Inc., 1964). The thrust of Aquinas' argument is to purchase a sense sufficiently definite to realize our intention of speaking of God without sacrificing the "infinite qualitative difference." In the spirit of Schleiermacher, Langdon Gilkey comes down on the other side, without, however, so careful an argument as Aquinas: "The way we understand the divine in each of the above is very much shaped by the unique 'meaning' or structure of the symbol; it is a *Christian* apprehension and understanding. But *what* we understand through these unique symbols and so in this unique way is the appearance of the sacred in and through the finite, and not the sacred by itself" (*Naming the Whirlwind: The Renewal of God Language* [The Bobbs-Merrill Company, Inc., 1969], pp. 466–467). The second sentence parts from Aquinas, not the first. One wonders why the adversative "but" introduces the second sentence. Gilkey's theory of reference seems to follow smoothly upon his remarks about meaning; it is Aquinas who needs to make an argument.

9. I have found corroboration for the critic analogy from Wilfred Cantwell Smith, *Questions of Religious Truth* (Charles Scribner's Sons, 1967): "The theologian is to revelation as a music critic to music" (p. 82). Northrop Frye engages in the perilous pursuit of norms for criticism in his *Anatomy of Criticism* (Princeton University Press, 1957), and the manner in which that book is forced to proceed as well as its uneasy reception indicates the paradoxical nature of the task itself. Henri deLubac's judgment, for example, that the eighteenth-century Louvain theologians "*ont perdu le sens de dieu*" is of a piece with literary critical assessments (Henri deLubac, *Surnaturel* [Paris: Aubier, 1946], pp. 33–37). The strength of the judgment can be measured by the success with which deLubac can show them losing sight of the "infinite qualitative difference" by the questions they ask and the kinds of inquiry they insist on pursuing. Hence it proves to be organization—syntax, roughly speaking—which provides grounds for assessments like these.

10. Gilkey has reminded us in a careful way that when philosophical theology cedes to the temptation of system to engage in arguments which purport to prove, the god which results "is thus a prisoner held by and hidden behind principles of thought more basic than himself. . . . The real ultimate or sacred, then, in such natural theologies is not the god that reason discovers by implication, but the ultimate coherence of the universe, or of process itself, which reason presupposes for its metaphysical vision" (*Naming*, p. 441).

11. Cf. my "Analogy and Judgment" in F. E. Crowe (ed.), *Spirit as Inquiry* (St. Xavier College, 1964 = *Continuum* 2 [1964]).

12. The lasting contribution of the *Tractatus Logico-Philosophicus* of Ludwig Wittgenstein will be, I take it, the rigorous examination of limits from *this* side. Cf. Note 23.

13. Bernard J. F. Lonergan's favorite example of doctrine in formation and of the historical consciousness required for doctrinal investigation is the Council of Nicaea; cf. "Christ as Subject: A Reply," in F. E. Crowe (ed.), *Collection: Papers* (Herder & Herder, Inc., 1967).

14. A most thorough yet suggestive and often tentative exploration of various language used in man's attempt to speak of and to God may be found in D. D. Evans, *Logic of Self-Involvement* (London: SCM Press, Ltd., 1965; Herder & Herder, Inc., 1969).

15. From my own explorations of the question of analogical language, I can cite "Religious Language and the Logic of Analogy," *Inter Phil. Quar.*, No. 2 (1962), pp. 643–658, "Aquinas on Naming God," *Theological Studies*, No. 24 (1963), pp. 183–212, and a full-length study soon to be published in book form.

16. Hence the controlling conviction of *all* of Wittgenstein's work, I believe: "The fact that the propositions of logic are tautologies *shows* the formal—logical—properties of language and the world" (*Tractatus* 6.12). Again, in the *Philosophical Investigations*: "How do I find the 'right' word? How do I choose among words? . . . I do not always have to make judgments, give explanations; often I might only say: 'It simply

isn't right yet.' I am dissatisfied, I go on looking. At last a word comes: 'that's it!' Sometimes I can say why. This is simply what searching, this is what finding, is like here" (p. 218).

17. This I find to be the crippling weakness of the "new hermeneutic" school: they feel that all must be said, and in this respect among others, are hardly new: notably, J. M. Robinson and J. B. Cobb (eds.), New Frontiers in Theology (Harper & Row, Publishers, Inc., 1963, 1965, 1967), especially Vol. I, The Later Heidegger and Theology, and Vol. II, The New Hermeneutic.

18. So, for example, Carnap thinks to avoid metaphysical issues by adjudging one's acceptance of this framework rather than that one to be "a practical, not a theoretical question. . . . The acceptance cannot be judged as being either true or false because it is not an assertion. It can only be judged as being more or less expedient, fruitful, conducive to the aim from which the language is intended" (Meaning and Necessity [The University of Chicago Press, 1956], p. 214), as though these other "facts" were settled more easily than "truth" or "falsity."

19. Heidegger's way of dealing with the history of philosophy involves a critical recognition of indebtedness. This proves to be a useful model for learning what it is to do philosophy in making the effort to assimilate another; cf. Introduction to Metaphysics (Doubleday & Company, Inc., 1961), pp. 45–58.

20. Frederick J. Streng, Emptiness: A Study in Religious Meaning (Abingdon Press, 1967).

21. W. V. O. Quine, Ontological Relativity (Columbia University Press, 1969), especially the first two chapters.

22. Albert Camus, The Myth of Sisyphus (Alfred A. Knopf, Inc., 1955), followed by more sophisticated essays on the same theme of meaning, notably The Rebel (Alfred A. Knopf, Inc., 1956).

23. Speaking of the Tractatus, Wittgenstein wrote to Ficker in 1919: "The book's point is an ethical one. . . . My work consists of two parts: the one presented here plus all that I have not written. And it is precisely this second part that is the important one. My book draws limits to the sphere of the ethical from the inside as it were, and I am convinced that this is the ONLY rigorous way of drawing those limits. In short, I believe that where many others today are just gassing, I have managed in my book to put everything firmly into place by being silent about it" (Paul Engelmann [ed.], Letters from Ludwig Wittgenstein [Oxford: Basil Blackwell & Mott, Ltd., 1967], p. 143).

24. The phrase is a conceit of Quine's: Ontological Relativity, p. 5.

25. Hegel and Wittgenstein each appreciated the logical "fact" about limits: to formulate them is to have transcended them, although each made of it something quite different. On "facts," cf. Edy Zemach, "Wittgenstein's Philosophy of the Mystical," Review of Metaphysics, No. 18 (1964), pp. 38–57, Part I.

26. Wittgenstein has recourse to the term "elucidation" when he must remark on the role that the statements of the Tractatus themselves play:

"The meanings of primitive signs can be explained by means of elucidations (*Erläuterungen*)" (3.263); "Philosophy is not a body of doctrine but an activity. A philosophical work consists essentially of elucidations (*Erläuterungen*)" (4.112); and in the penultimate elucidation: "My propositions serve as elucidations (*erlautern dadurch*) in the following way." (6.54).

27. Early evidence of Wittgenstein's premonitions about the centrality of *use* appears in the construction of 2.1. in the *Tractatus*: "We picture facts to ourselves (*Wir machen uns Bilder der Tatsachen*)." The more one accents the *we* who picture, the more he becomes conscious that we do so for a purpose.

28. Aristotle gives many cogent reasons for *not* taking his *Metaphysics* as a science, especially in Book III, but the single slip in proposing it as *proto-episteme* in Book VI seemed to carry the weight in traditional presentations. Preller argues (in *Divine Science*) that all forms of knowing about something, all articulating of what is the case, is for Aquinas "by analogy" (pp. 69–72).

29. Gilkey, again, in summary reference to his own previous analysis, notes that "we found that every god of natural theology is established as 'real' by the categories of a metaphysical system; if he is thus dependent on them for his reality and intelligibility, he can hardly then transcend those categories once he appears on the scene" (*Naming*, p. 441). Nor does Gilkey's criticism amount to a wholesale rejection of "natural theology"; he argues for another use of philosophical theology which would be served were philosophy to achieve its aim of "sheer disclosure." The aim is articulated by Whitehead in *Modes of Thought* (The Macmillan Company, 1948), p. 67, and cited in Gilkey (*Naming*, p. 440, n. 15); yet part of the force of my critique is that Whitehead failed to achieve this aim precisely because he was unable to view philosophy as other than a most general theory. The distinction between proposition and elucidation is necessary to allow words to disclose without proposing yet another system.

30. Cf. my "How Complete Can Intelligibility Be? A Commentary on Insight XIX" in *Proceedings of the American Catholic Philological Association*, 1967; and John S. Dunne, *A Search for God in Time and Memory* (The Macmillan Company, 1969), on Socratic ignorance.

3

The Alienated Theologian

VAN A. HARVEY

Der Mensch hat den Trieb, gegen die Grenzen der Sprache anzurennen. Denken Sie, z.B., an das Erstaunen, dass etwas existiert. Das Erstaunen kann nicht in Form einer Frage ausgedruckt werden, und es gibt auch gar keine Antwort. Alles, was wir sagen mögen, kann a priori nur Unsinn sein. Trotzdem rennen wir gegen die Grenzen der Sprache an. (Wittgenstein to Schlick, 1929.)

I

One of the most striking characteristics of Protestant theology in the last two centuries has been the emergence of what I shall call the alienated theologian, the professional who is concerned with the articulation of the faith of the Christian community but who is himself as much a doubter as a believer. This is a new phenomenon in the history of Christendom, because it has always been assumed that the Christian theologian was a believer who differed from other believers only by virtue of his office to clarify and defend the Christian faith. But beginning with the Christian deists in the eighteenth century and culminating in the radical theologians of the last decade, we see the Christian theologian gradually accepting the premises of the unbelief it has always been his office to overcome. Sometimes his doubt and alienation are not severe—when, for example, the liberal theologian finds himself unable to accept some marginal doctrine or belief. Sometimes the doubt is more serious—when the theologian doubts the truth of the resurrection belief or can make no sense out of the incarnation. One might say that the history of Protestant theology in the last century is the history of these milder and more serious forms of alienated theology.

In the last decade, however, there has emerged a more radical doubt among Protestant theologians, a doubt that poses fundamental questions for the church concerning the future of theology itself. This radical doubt is most apparent among the so-called "death of God" theologians, although it is not restricted to them. In them, the dubiety is not so much about marginal doctrine as about the essence of faith itself: the existence of God. What makes this new phenomenon especially interesting is that these professional theologians do not leave the Christian community or give up theology. They are still preoccupied with the significance of Jesus Christ for human life, and they read and comment on the work of other more orthodox theologians. Nevertheless, they are deeply estranged from the faith, and their work reflects this estrangement. They are "unhappy lovers" of Christian theology.

So far, I have spoken quite generally of the alienated theologian, but a look at the chaotic scene in contemporary theology discloses quite diverse types of alienation. There are those who are strident and humorless in their attempts to pour the new atheistic wine into the old wineskins. There are others who proceed with more urbanity and wit. At home in the secular world of technology and sex, they offer piecemeal attempts to bring Christianity into conformity with the Zeitgeist. There are others who, though alienated, believe they can reconcile themselves to the historic faith by means of a metaphysical translation of some sort. There are still others who are not easily characterized.

In such a confused situation as this, perhaps an allegory may

be permitted. Imagine the Christian community to be like the
Children of Israel who, wandering across the desolate waste-
lands, believe God has miraculously delivered them from the
fleshpots of Egypt and now sustains them with the manna from
heaven and the pillar of fire. The Israelites huddle about their
campfires at night and sing the praises of their deliverer. On
the edges of the camp, there are some stragglers. They were
once Israelites but, for various reasons, they have become dis-
enchanted. They stay alive by picking up the crumbs of the
manna left over by the Children of Israel, and at night they
warm themselves at the outer edges of the campfires. But they
do not like the songs the Israelites sing, and they find the
evening sermons dull and filled with cheap apologetics. The
stragglers only seem to become involved when they are drawn
into theological debate with the more sophisticated of the
Israelites. The pattern of these debates, however, is often disturbing to the more pious Israelites. Some of the stragglers, for
example, say something like this: "Your Israelite beliefs are
incredible if taken at face value. But happily one doesn't have
to so take them because analysis reveals that what you are
really saying is more profound. You are really expressing a moral
policy to act as if there were a deliverer and as if there were a
fiery pillar." This translation not only perplexes the Israelites
but angers other stragglers who retort: "That translation does
not make any sense at all. It simply does not do justice to the
metaphysics of the matter. Actually, the Israelites have two
metaphysical beliefs embedded in their mythology and these
must be distinguished, although the Israelites, of course, have
confused them. One belief has to do with God as an efficient
causal power, as symbolized by the miraculous deliverance from
Egypt. The other belief refers to God as a lure, a presenter of
possibility, which is symbolized nicely by the pillar of fire. Now,
the first belief rests on a bad conception of power. The second
belief contains a more adequate conception because the 'power
that counts is the power to influence the exercise of power by

others.' " [1] This statement in turn precipitates a heated debate among the stragglers, so heated and prolonged that most of the Israelites lose interest and slip away to their tents.

When they are back in their tents, the Israelites confess that they are impressed with the profundity of some of the translations that have been offered, but they also confess that they do not recognize their beliefs in them. "What would it mean," one asks, "to say that there is no deliverer and no pillar but that we are committed to acting as if there were?" "Yes," says another, "and if real power is the ability to influence the exercise of power by others, what kind of power is it that the others have that is to be influenced? Is it the old-fashioned kind of power or the power to influence the influencer?" [2] Still, the Israelites cannot find it in their hearts to reject the stragglers. Moreover, they think it might prove useful when the time comes to send the stragglers on ahead to the Canaanites when the latter hold their annual Religious Emphasis Week. At least the stragglers might convince the Canaanites that the Israelite faith deserves their intellectual respect.

There is one theologian of great prestige among the Israelites —he is called Saul, son of Tillich—who argues that the stragglers ought not to feel so alienated. One night in a powerful address on what it means to be a theologian he argues that the first condition for being a true theologian is to doubt whether there is a deliverer or a fiery pillar and that he who claims he is confident there is a deliverer and a pillar should not be accepted as a theologian. Thus, even if one feels himself estranged from the community, he should be accepted as its spokesman if he asks the question of the community's ultimate concern, for it is this ultimate concern which constitutes the identity of Israel.[3] Therefore, Tillich invites the stragglers to join the body of wanderers.

This invitation is eagerly accepted by some of the stragglers, but one or two others hang back. "Why are you hanging back?" they are asked. One of the stragglers answers: "Because I think the invitation to join is a seduction and ought to be resisted.

In the first place, it ought to be resisted for the sake of the integrity of the Israelite community itself. A community of faith cannot long survive in the desert if there are no commonly accepted norms to which the community can appeal if disputes and controversy arise. Every community is rooted in some common vision of reality, some orthodoxy, however defined. Therefore, it is demoralizing to have its spokesman say that its real meaning is something other than what the members of that community have always said its meaning is. It is as though a Marxist philosopher were to insist that the real meaning of the *Manifesto* is free enterprise, or as if a spokesman for the SDS were to say that membership was open to the military-industrial complex. In the second place, I think the invitation to join the community is a threat to our own integrity as individual thinkers. If we join, we will always be tempted to bend our thought to make it acceptable to the Israelites. This is neither good philosophy nor good theology. The truth is that we are spiritual parasites who live vicariously off the faith of the Israelite faith. Perhaps it would simply be better to confess this and to go on as we are, as alienated theologians. If we join the community, we may destroy it, and then we will all be homeless wanderers on the face of the desert."

This reply, surprisingly enough, has the effect of unifying many of the stragglers with many of the Israelites. They argue that this view defines the Israelites in terms which are too static, in terms of dogma and belief, and thus raises once again the undemocratic specter of heresy, a word the Israelites have not used since they left Egypt. "Call yourself anything you like," they shout after the lonely straggler, "but we will call you an effete philosopher of religion." This appellation stuns the alienated theologian because he does not understand himself to be a philosopher of religion in any of the usual senses of that term. He is not interested in tracing the logic of religious language nor in building up some kind of synthetic truth that embraces all religions. He is preoccupied with the faith of Israel, and he wants desperately to make some sense out of it for himself. It is the faith of this community that haunts him. He is an "unhappy lover" and he is looking for a style of thought and life that expresses the pathos of his situation.

No discussion of the future of philosophical theology can long ignore the phenomenon of the alienated theologian, for his very existence poses fundamental questions concerning the aims, substance, and style of Christian theology in our time. Therefore, I wish to take the opportunity given to me at this Consultation to offer some reflections on this matter. I wish to explore what Kierkegaard would have called the pathos of the alienated theologian's situation: the reasons, psychological and logical, for his alienation; the kinds of problems with which he necessarily finds himself wrestling, and the style in which this best finds expression. In defense of this more personal and wide-ranging project, I take refuge behind the shield of the invitation originally given to the speakers by our host, namely, that we write programmatic essays, by which I understand something less technical than might normally be expected from one who is called a philosophical theologian. I do not mean to suggest by this that you should be less critical than you might otherwise be; I am only trying to make clear in advance what I propose to do.

II

The various forms of intellectual alienation in the modern world from the Christian faith are unintelligible, as I have argued at length elsewhere,[4] without having understood the moral dimensions of religious doubt and how these moral dimensions are a function of a morality of knowledge that, since the Enlightenment, has progressively dominated the consciousness of the Western intellectual. This morality of knowledge is capable of being described in many ways but it embodies such virtues as skepticism against unfounded assertions, the suspicion

of irrational authority, the prizing of logical candor, the appeal
to evidence, and the careful qualification of one's claims. This
morality first found expression in the eighteenth-century ideal
of the reasonable man or the "lover of truth," the unerring
mark of which was, as John Locke argued, the "not entertaining
any proposition with greater assurance than the proofs it is
built upon will warrant." [5] The same ideal was formulated more
negatively but stridently by W. K. Clifford in the nineteenth
century when he wrote that "it is wrong, always, everywhere,
and for anyone, to believe anything on insufficient evidence." [6]

This ideal, even when so formally stated, sounds radical
enough when set against the background of the ethics of belief
of traditional Christendom, which may be said to have regarded
credulity and belief as virtues and skepticism as a sin. But the
revolutionary implications of the new morality of knowledge did
not become apparent until it became linked to the pursuit of
knowledge within professionalized spheres of inquiry such as
astronomy, physics, sociology, psychology, and history, and informed the educational policy of the schools and universities
that became the guardians of these professionalized spheres. In
this way, the new ethics of belief became rooted in one of the
most important institutions shaping the modern secular spirit.
Everyone aspired to be educated and all educated men were to
be taught, as G. M. Young put the matter, that a man had no
more right to an opinion for which he could not account than
for a pint of beer for which he could not pay.[7] To account for
an opinion was to master the evidence and the arguments per-
taining to knowledge in a specific sphere of inquiry. In the
eighteenth century one could appeal quite abstractly to reason;
but in the twentieth century, this appeal is known to be quite
empty until located in some concrete context, some specialized
or logical field.[8] One might say that the virtues of skepticism,
evidence, logical candor, assessment, and qualified judgment
are field-invariant but that the warrants and backings of concrete arguments are all field-dependent.

The close relationship of the morality of knowledge to the specialization of knowledge is crucial for analyzing the problem of religious doubt, especially that of the alienated theologian. For the sophisticated doubter does not doubt wholesale, so to speak, but retail, and whether his doubt has a moral component is closely related to the specificity of the belief in question, its logical field, so to speak. One may put the matter this way. The alienated theologian sees the Christian faith as a network of belief woven together out of many logically diverse strands. The Christian faith contains many different kinds of claims. It contains historical, anthropological, ontological, cosmological, and normative as well as theological claims. The monolithic sounding "the Christian faith" tends to blur these logical distinctions, to suggest that all the claims are of one sort. But because they are not of one logical sort, the doubts with respect to each of them must be analyzed differently. For example, no problem of moral integrity will arise concerning a concrete religious belief unless it involves a claim that is untenable within a specific field of inquiry or that requires a degree of assent that is not justifiable by the standards of that inquiry. Suppose the alienated theologian has doubts about the existence of God and also thinks that this belief does not impinge on any specific and professionalized field of knowledge. This doubt will not involve a matter of integrity in the same way, say, that his doubt concerning the Mosaic authorship of the Pentateuch does, because the latter does involve a collision with a professional sphere of knowledge, namely, Old Testament history and criticism.

It is against this background that one can best understand and analyze the theological problems that Biblical criticism posed for the liberal Christian in the nineteenth century and still does for the alienated theologian. The emergence of historical inquiry as a professionalized sphere of knowledge with its own canons and rules of inquiry deprived, in effect, the church of any cognitive authority with respect to historical claims. If one believed that what the church said about any given event of the past was true, one did so not because the church said it but because independent historical investigation justified it. Insofar, however, as the traditional Christian faith did seem to depend on certain historical claims, whether these were justified by historical investigation or not, the alienated theologian came to believe that this faith corroded the delicate machinery of critical historical judgment. The believer's use of Biblical sources, his ambivalent and contradictory attitudes toward present knowledge and its role in historical judgment, his special pleading, the heavy assent given to propositions deserving at most only light assent—all these led the alienated theologian to distrust religious faith insofar as it impinged on historical inquiry.[9] More important, however, the alienated theologian himself came to reject those historical claims made about Jesus that have always been part and parcel of traditional Christian belief: his miraculous birth, life, and resurrection from the dead. Moreover, he even became skeptical of many of those assertions about Jesus that more liberal versions of Christianity—such as those of Tillich, the New Quest, and the Theology of Hope—believe to be absolutely fundamental.[10]

If you have followed my argument so far, you may have been tempted to reply in terms something like this:

> Well, if that is all your alienation amounts to, I am both relieved and amused. Relieved, because I expected something more radical; amused, because you are actually so conservative. Granted that you may have intellectual difficulties with the historical beliefs of Christianity, these difficulties need not lead to any profound alienation. No really important contemporary Protestant theologian, for example, has lost much sleep over the question of the historicity of the resurrection of Jesus or of his Messianic self-consciousness. Brunner, Bultmann, Tillich, the Niebuhrs—all believed in a righteous God, which is really the

crucial issue, without committing themselves to untenable historical claims. And since the belief in God does not involve any conflict with a specific field of knowledge, to use your terms, no moral problem need arise.

This reply has, to be sure, some cogency, but it fails to take account of the fact that some of the more deeply alienated Protestant theologians were teethed and raised on the writings of just these neo-orthodox theologians and only reached their present stage of alienation when they became convinced that this theology was tenable only so long as its basic ambiguity concerning the relationship of faith to historical judgments about Jesus went unanalyzed. More formally expressed, the alienated theologian became convinced that the neo-orthodox theologians had not seen as clearly as the orthodox had the logical lines of connections between belief in a righteous God and historical claims about the life of Jesus. On the one hand, the neo-orthodox theologian claimed to speak of a decisive revelation in Jesus Christ as the only basis of confidence in the existence of a righteous God. On the other hand, he described the content of Christian faith in such a radical fashion—one thinks especially of the early Barth, or Bultmann, and the Tillich of *The Courage to Be*—that this faith was consistent with theoretical atheism! [11] Once it became clear to the alienated theologian that historical inquiry could not sustain the Christological base and that the radical faith in the "God beyond God" had little intrinsic relation to this base, the question arose whether this faith was specifically Christian or whether it could be best formulated in theistic terms at all.

At this point it might be argued that the dilemma of the Protestant alienated theologian is merely a function of having initially embraced a theology that made the error of trying to erect its belief in God on a purely Christological base. But surely, it will be said, there are at least three other alternatives and all of them are more tenable so far as the ethics of belief are concerned. The first of these alternatives is that belief concerning the existence of God is not based on Christology alone but on a metaphysics of some kind, whether it be a classical or a more contemporary form like that, say, of process philosophy. This alternative has the merit of apparently meeting the objection that belief in God violates the rule that one should have reasons for one's theological convictions. There are reasons but they are metaphysical reasons. The second alternative is fideism and lies at the other end of the spectrum so far as the morality of knowledge is concerned. For fideism rejects the enterprise of metaphysics as a legitimate form of knowledge and argues that belief in God is a leap of faith. Nevertheless, the fideist also believes that his position has intellectual integrity because there can be no collision between faith and metaphysics if the latter is not a legitimate form of knowledge. Therefore, one is morally free to make the leap. The third alternative is to say that belief in God is rooted in man's religious experience, either in mystical experience or in basic human experiences of contingency, ultimacy, and the sacred.[12] This alternative also has the merit of turning aside the moral objections to religious belief because the experience itself constitutes a reason for believing. Religious symbols may be regarded as ways of thematizing these basic elements in human experience.

It is obviously impossible within the limited scope of this paper to deal at all adequately with the issues raised by these three alternatives. All I can attempt to do is sketch in rather roughhewn terms the outlines of the situation as it looks to my not-so-mythical alienated theologian. I shall deal with the first and second alternatives briefly and postpone a discussion of the third until later in my paper, for reasons that will, I hope, become clear.

The difficulty the alienated theologian has with metaphysics as the basis for religious belief is rooted in his dubiety about the enterprise itself, a dubiety he shares with a great number of contemporary philosophers. Many reasons can be given for this dubiety but the most obvious one arises as one confronts the radical and fundamental disagreements among metaphysicians themselves regarding almost every aspect of their enterprise: its definition, the categories that are to be used, the kinds of warrants that will license inference, the data, and the logical status of the conclusions that are forthcoming. These differences are so profound that they inevitably raise the question whether the enterprise should be called a specialized sphere of knowledge at all in contrast to speculative play or belief. Actually, as several philosophers have themselves pointed out, the alienated theologian thinks it important to make a distinction between two types of metaphysics: one that is primarily concerned with developing an explanatory hypothesis for the existence of the world and the way things are in it, and one that may be said to be more descriptive, that is, an attempt to clarify and to give a unified account of the fundamental presuppositions of human experience.[13] Now, the alienated theologian has important reservations about the status of descriptive metaphysics, but he regards explanatory metaphysics as a highly refined and imaginative but nevertheless speculative form of belief. And because it is, he does not see what justifies the hard assent to the conclusions that arise from it, an assent which seems implied by Christian faith, for Christian faith seems to be, at least in its traditional form, a type of explanatory or transcendental metaphysics. It postulates a cause for the world and a reason for the way things are, including the course of history.

The usual reply to this is that it is a psychological rather than a logical argument, that it simply reflects a sophomoric paralysis in the face of the plethora of metaphysical systems. Like the beginning student of philosophy who is immobilized by the succession of philosophical systems—Plato's, Aristotle's, Leibniz's, Hegel's, Spinoza's, Bergson's, Whitehead's, Heidegger's—the alienated theologian is not sophisticated enough to see that one of these possibilities might, nevertheless, be true.

I am not at all sure the problem of metaphysical pluralism can be so easily dismissed or that the psychology of the matter can be so nicely differentiated from its logic, any more than the psychological feeling "I'm sure" can so neatly be separated from the linguistic setting in which one can justify the use of "I know." [14] The term "I know," in contrast to "I believe" normally occurs in situations, as J. L. Austin has shown, in which the speaker puts forward a claim with authority, that is, with the assurance that his word is especially reliable. To say that it is reliable is to say that he could, if challenged, produce grounds of the highest relevancy and cogency for his judgment, that the data and warrants justify his claim. What these grounds are will, of course, vary from field to field. But what will not vary regardless of the field is that the warrants which license his inferences and which give a certain force to his conclusion will be shared warrants, in short, that they be matters of agreement. Indeed, as Stephen Toulmin has pointed out, unless we tacitly assume some warrants in any given field, it will be impossible to submit any argument in that field to rational assessment. "We should not even know what sort of data were of the slightest relevance to a conclusion, if we had not at least a provisional idea of the warrants acceptable in the situation confronting us." [15] To say, "I believe," on the other hand, is to say that we believe something to be true but are also aware that the shared reasons do not justify the stronger "I know" or, perhaps, that the reasons are not shared. Knowing, in other words, is tied to consensus and social corroboration.

It is in this context that the disagreements and conflicts among speculative metaphysicians raise epistemological questions of a serious sort, for these disagreements are not intramural in the sense, say, that the conflict between two biologists' causal explanations are intramural. The differences are more fundamental. They arise over such matters as the nature of language and logic and the choice of the basic categories to be used. The arguments swirl around such questions as whether "the world exists" is a necessary or a contingent proposition, whether the world can be identified demonstrably or not, whether the universe is an occurrence or a regularity, whether the term "the universe" functions as a concept or a proper noun, whether the principle of sufficient reason is valid or not, not to mention the status of existence claims and the principle of causality and the justification of inference itself.[16] These issues are so complex and problematical and there are so many first-rate philosophers aligned on almost every side of each issue that it strikes the alienated theologian as comic (in the Kierkegaardian sense) to employ the words "I know" in these matters. There seems to be no way to adjudicate the issues or even to know how one might go about getting agreement on the principles of adjudication. The psychology of the matter is not unrelated to its logic.

Now, it is important to understand that the alienated theologian is not claiming that speculative or explanatory metaphysics is an illegitimate enterprise, because he has no interest in ruling out speculation or any other intellectual activity men wish to engage in. Rather, he is saying that he finds agnosticism with respect to the claims of explanatory metaphysics to be more responsible in his case than assent. Therefore, he does not see how metaphysics can provide the basis for Christian belief because he does not think that Christian belief is compatible with such agnosticism. It is just this which constitutes a stumbling block to his joining the main body of believers.

Since the work of Immanuel Kant, the fideistic solution has attempted to exploit this metaphysical agnosticism. To limit reason was to make room for faith. Thus Kierkegaard could argue that speculative metaphysics should be regarded as merely an experiment in thought; to believe it makes the philosopher a comic figure. The existing individual must make a lonely leap of faith, and since this leap of faith violates no rules of acquiring knowledge, the moral objections to it are groundless. One might interpret many of the important religious philosophies since the mid-nineteenth century—those of Newman, Kierkegaard, James, Troeltsch, Ritschl, Herrmann—as a series of attempts to justify the right to believe given the rejection of metaphysics. On philosophical grounds, there is much to be said for some of their proposals. Nevertheless, their solution poses peculiar problems for the alienated theologian. The first of these is what is logically meant by a leap of faith, especially when faith is identified with believing propositions of some sort, paradoxical or otherwise. On the surface at least, it is not clear that it makes sense to try to make a leap of belief, for believing is not the sort of thing one can try to do. Believing, unlike leaping, is not under the immediate and voluntary control of the will. One can, to be sure, plead with a child in a burning building to attempt a leap to safety, perhaps even to trust his father to catch him, and one can shout to a drowning man to try to swim to the shore, but to one perplexed about the existence of God or about the truth of a proposition, does it make any sense to say, "But just try to believe"? I think not. One might say, perhaps, "Consider this evidence" or, "Look in this direction" or, "Entertain this argument" but not, "Just try to believe." This is, I am aware, a very complicated issue and I have attempted to deal with it elsewhere,[17] but if my view is reasonable then one would have to say that the arguments advanced by William James[18] and, more recently, Diogenes Allen,[19] might possibly be regarded as reasons given after the fact of believing but ineffective as reasons to invoke belief. Pascal, I believe, was closer to the truth in seeing the analogies between believing and betting, but once again there are important differences, for betting does not carry with it the psychological assurance of believing, and it is just this assurance that the religious believer has and which the alienated theologian wants but does not have and that accounts for his being a straggler at all.

III

If these alternatives appear so unfruitful to the alienated theologian, then it seems fair to ask why he continues to be a straggler at all. Surely it cannot be because, like the stragglers in my allegory, there is no place to go, because whatever else it may be like, modern secular culture is not like a desert. Indeed, the alienated theologian who advances an imaginative translation of the faith these days is apt to find his picture in *Time* magazine and his essays and paperbacks widely distributed by college chaplains and youth leaders. He may even be invited to sit in an endowed chair in the department of religion of some prestigious secular university at a salary (bread) which, by comparison, reveals the manna of the Israelite theologian to be the crumbs they are.

There are, no doubt, complex psychological reasons in each alienated theologian's case, and I do not believe it fruitful to generalize too much about the psychology of the stragglers. I can offer you, however, the reflections and reasonings of one kind of camp follower. These reasonings, it will become clear, are of different logical sorts and some of them may strike you as peculiarly lacking in force. But I thought it might prove useful to me, if not to you, to articulate these as clearly as I can and to see whether they can survive the scrutiny you will undoubtedly give them.

The first reason may seem so commonplace and banal as to be scarcely worth mentioning, especially in this age when every reason is advanced by contemporary theologians for being a Christian except that Christian beliefs are true. The alienated theologian cannot completely stifle the possibility that the beliefs of the Israelites may be true or, at least, a confused way of articulating some awareness of a reality that men are otherwise blind to. It is possible that despite the dogmatism and the *Aberglaube*—indeed, perhaps in and through the *Aberglaube*—the Israelites are witnesses to something immensely important for human life. He is aware that if this is the case it would not be the first time in human history in which the truth has been intuited through a vehicle that was inadequate to it. And who can be so sure that the Israelite beliefs are false? The alienated theologian finds the metaphysical arguments of the anti-theists no more deserving of heavy assent than the metaphysical arguments of the theists. He does not think that any absolutely devastating arguments have yet been advanced against the belief in the existence of a benevolent deity, and as an explanatory hypothesis for the existence of the world, it seems to be no worse, though no better, than many of the hypotheses cast up by unbelieving philosophers. The difficulty is that the alienated theologian cannot regard the belief in God merely as a speculative hypothesis that he can entertain as abstractly as he does other explanatory hypotheses. It may date him, but he finds himself in agreement with John Henry Newman when Newman said that he could not understand those who treated the proposition "There may be a God" with the same indifference with which they treat the proposition "A murder has just been committed in Japan." [20]

But if, as I have argued, it does not seem possible to settle the issue, if the question concerning the existence of God is an unanswerable question on the basis of anything we now know, then what point is there in pursuing it? This leads me to consider another reason for being a straggler, a reason that is very difficult for certain intellectuals in our culture to understand, much less appreciate. It is difficult for them to understand because they believe that unanswerable questions are, by definition, meaningless questions. Here, however, the metaphor of the desert may not be altogether inappropriate. Every mind has, so to speak, its own desert, and for one type of alienated theologian at least, this secular culture of ours with its unbounded confidence in technology, sex, and science and the meaninglessness of the unanswerable question is not unlike a wasteland. Therefore, he believes it important for the consciousness of man— or, at least, for his own consciousness—that one struggle with those fundamental mysteries at the borders of thought that humble and perplex us and call into question our basic attitude toward life itself.

There are many such mysteries or, perhaps, aspects of one basic mystery. The alienated theologian may be struck by the astonishment that anything should exist at all. He is aware that some philosophers think this a confused and meaningless sort of astonishment; but, on the other hand, he also knows that some of the greatest philosophical minds of the West have been led to formulate this astonishment in the form of a question, Is there a reason for the existence of the universe? and that other philosophers have argued cogently that this is a meaningful question.[21] Moreover, the alienated theologian, following Wittgenstein, may see inner connections between this astonishment and the pervasiveness of order and the intelligibility of this order.[22] He is impressed in ways that he can scarcely articulate by the way in which the necessities of mathematics and logic seem to lay some purchase on this reality. He does not find the appeal to the process of evolution explanatory and he cannot agree with Nietzsche that the order we experience is merely the arbitrary projection of the human mind over a chaotic and formless experience.

The alienated theologian is impressed with the fantastic fecundity of being and this, in turn, seems to be closely related to a feeling he scarcely knows how to express or articulate—the sacredness of life and being and the incredible beauty of it all. He is struck by his affinity with those thinkers such as Loren Eiseley who are also haunted by this mystery. In his recent book, *The Unexpected Universe*, Eiseley tells of how he lay one hot humid night in his room in Costabel staring abstractedly at the ceiling, when he became conscious of a commotion on the beach outside. The tides of a recent storm had thrown up millions of aquatic creatures—octopuses, crabs, starfish—and the professional shellers were scurrying about with their flares competing frantically and lustfully with one another for them. As a disinterested naturalist, Eiseley arose to observe the great collection. Suddenly depressed at the sight of this life rejected by the mother of all life, the sea, and by the greedy madness of the collectors, he walked up the beach only to see a lonely figure who, unlike the others, was gently picking up the dying star-fish and flinging them back into the sea. Approaching the lonely star-thrower, he heard him say: "The stars throw well. One can help them." The naturalist remained for a while and then made his way back through the greedy collectors to his room, where he tossed fitfully and reflected on the immense journey man himself had made from the sea, the aeons of life-and-death struggles in the bogs of primeval swamps. But he could not repress the image of the star-thrower. Somehow, he thought,

> From Darwin's tangled bank of unceasing struggle, self-ishness, and death, had arisen, incomprehensibly, the thrower who loved not man, but life. It was the subtle cleft in nature before which biological thinking had faltered. We had reached the last shore of an invisible island—yet, strangely, also a shore that the primitives had always known. They had sensed intuitively that man cannot exist spiritually without life, his brother, even if he slays him. Somewhere, my thought persisted, there is a hurler of stars, and he walks, because he chooses, always in desolation, but not in defeat.[23]

Eiseley's reflections force us to the awareness of the discontinuities of the unexpected universe, of the "rents in nature" that raise the haunting possibility of there being a star-thrower who redeems all human star-throwing from the meaningless-ness and absurdity of Sisyphus. The alienated theologian, like Eiseley, wishes to align himself with the star-throwers. He is outraged at man's exploitation of other forms of life. He finds some powerful compulsion in Dostoevsky's vision that we are all responsible for the earth. He finds it somehow inadequate to say that man should preserve the other creatures for the utilitarian reason that other men might enjoy them. He feels that these creatures ought to exist even if no other men ever enjoy them. He hardly knows how to articulate these feelings except in the categories of the sacred. He does not regard these feelings as grounds for believing in the existence of God, but he also knows that the existence of God is compatible with such feelings— perhaps even suggested by them—and because of this, he is drawn to wrestle with the themes that preoccupy the religious community. For the religious community is a perpetual reminder to Egyptians, Canaanites, rationalistic Greeks, and Philistines that there are dark and mysterious borders to our existence and that no man can control the manna which prompts a nameless gratitude that can alter our ways of looking at the world.

Since these sorts of experiences are closely related to a form of life in which one's attitude toward the world is transformed, the alienated theologian increasingly finds himself concerned with forms of religious experience and their interpretation. This concern is not without its ironies, because the alienated Protestant theologian, at least, began his pilgrimage in the company of neo-orthodox theologians whose purpose was to repudiate the preoccupation with religious experience that had characterized Protestant theology since Schleiermacher. To some extent he has come back full circle to the beginnings of the nineteenth century. This return, however, is not mindless, because he sees that religious experience and its interpretation is directly related to the psychology and the logic of his position, grounded as it is in his morality of knowledge. Psychologically, the alienated theologian is envious of the subjective certitude that characterizes the self-consciousness of the religious believer, and logically he is aware that the enjoyment of a religious experience of some kind tends to set aside some of the force of the moral objection that can be leveled at a great deal of religious believing. For the fact is that a person who has a compelling experience is surely in a more tenable moral position as regards his believing than one who confesses that his believing is a leap of faith. If, for example, a witness in a court of law were to say that he believed that the defendant committed a murder but, under cross-examination, were to confess that he had no basis for his accusation, that the belief was simply a leap of faith, he would be intellectually irresponsible in a way that a witness would not be were he to say that he thought he had seen the defendant commit the act. He might be mistaken but he would not be culpable, especially if the alleged experience was so powerful as to have shaken him.

Moreover, religious experience often has interesting logical connections with the whole framework of religious belief. This is, of course, a complicated matter, but suppose we consider that a religion, formally regarded, is a kind of symbolic framework cast over the structures of existence and, therefore, a way of apprehending the world, a way of "seeing as," to use Wittgenstein's phrase. The religious symbolism refers in interesting ways to formal features of existence such as order and contingency and the patterns of human life. A religious experience of some powerful kind might then provide the suggestion, to use William Christian's term, that is the cause or the occasion for adopting some way of looking at and interpreting the world.[24] If one experiences bliss or happiness consequent upon his experience, this will naturally function psychologically, though not logically, to confirm the validity of the vision. Now, I am not claiming that religious experience always functions in this way, since it is also the case that some religious experiences are only interpreted as *religious* experiences if the person has already adopted some religious interpretation. I am only saying that a powerful religious experience can function as a suggestion, as an occasion or cause for adopting a religious perspective and an attitude toward the world or, if not that, for being more appreciative of such religious perspectives. One can find such experiences described in William James's *The Varieties of Religious Experience*.[25] These experiences seem to have occurred quite unexpectedly to persons who were not otherwise religious, and they functioned to jolt them into adopting a religious interpretation. B. F. McGuinness argues that some such experience seems to have happened to Wittgenstein and altered his way of looking at the world and made him more appreciative of traditional religious visions.[26]

One may even go so far as to say that the claim of a person to have had such a profound religious experience may constitute a reason for another person to think that the experience has some foundation in reality. If one wants to understand William James's own preoccupation with religious belief and its possible validity, he can best do this, I think, not by considering the arguments in his essay *The Will to Believe* but by analyzing the logic of his *Varieties*, a logic that is quickly and rather poignantly recapitulated in the answers he gave to a questionnaire submitted to him by J. P. Pratt.[27] The questions and answers are revealing not only of James's position but of the pathos of his own form of religious alienation.

Q. Why do you believe in God? Is it from some argument?
A. Emphatically, no.
Q. Or because you have experienced his presence?
A. No, but rather because I need it, so that it "must" be true.
Q. Or from authority, such as that of the Bible or of some prophetic person?
A. Only the whole tradition of religious people, to which something in me makes admiring response.
Q. Or from any other reason?
A. Only from the social reasons.
Q. Is God very real to you, as real as an earthly friend?
A. Dimly [real] not [as an earthly friend].
Q. Do you feel that you have experienced his presence?
A. Never.
Q. If you have had no such experience, do you accept the testimony of others who claim to have felt God's presence directly?
A. Yes! The whole line of testimony on this point is so strong that I am unable to pooh-pooh it away! No

doubt there is a germ in me of something similar that makes admiring response.

The problem here, of course, is how religious experience is to be interpreted, for no experience bears its own interpretation on its face. We are all aware, in the case of mystical experience, that though these experiences have certain formal characteristics in common, they are also interpreted quite differently depending upon the culture and the perceptual sets of the persons having them. James, as well as W. T. Stace,[28] both report mystical experiences had by atheists who, nevertheless, persisted in their atheism. One cannot, therefore, simply appeal to mystical experience as evidence for a transcendent reality of some kind.

The alienated theologian is only too aware of this; indeed, it is just his recognition of the plurality of possible ways of symbolizing and describing the world or any given experience that underlies his attitude toward metaphysics. It is just because he believes that conceptual systems are relative to purpose, aims, and interests that opens the door to a philosophical possibility other than theism, on the one hand, or atheism, on the other, a possibility in which a religious form of life is compatible with a theological agnosticism. I use the term "possibility" here because this constitutes an area I am still exploring rather than a position which I am ready to adopt. Let me see if I can sketch the issue in its rough outlines.

Perhaps the question concerning the reference for the term "God" can best be approached not by asking the question whether there is a transcendent being with certain attributes which is required as an explanatory hypothesis for the existence of the world but by asking whether there are certain kinds of experiences, such as mystical experiences, which are of such a kind as to make it natural to use the language of presence, a language in which it is natural to employ the second person pronoun "Thou." Let's call this, for the time being, first-order language. If one analyzes the language used by saints and mystics to articulate this experience, one discovers that this first-order language is sometimes used at the same time that they issue proscriptions against conceptualization. Let's call this conceptualization second-order discourse. The issue is whether this use of the second person pronoun, or the language of presence, together with a rejection of second-order conceptionalization is philosophically significant or not. It might prove useful to explore this, to see if the first-order expressions can be taken seriously in abstraction from the second-order theory-laden terms which very soon come to be regarded as ingredient in the experience itself.

Consider for purposes of illustration our experience with other persons. Let us accept for the moment that there is something valid in Martin Buber's distinction between an I-Thou relation and an I-It relation. I am aware that this twofold division of experience is problematic in certain respects but these difficulties, I believe, don't seriously prejudice what follows. The relationship of being caught up momentarily in a depth relationship that is so personal and unique and freighted with feelings and felt obligations naturally evokes the second person pronoun "you." In this "game situation," so to speak, the terms "I," "myself," "you," and "yourself" are naturally at home. This first-order discourse, however, seems compatible with a wide range of second-order theories of explanation. One may, for example, experience the depth relationship but attempt to explain it, as has classically been the case, by appeal to an immortal soul or, more recently, to a self. The depth relationship in itself does not seem to dictate any given second-order theory or even require that we give up some of those we have adopted for certain scientific purposes and aims.

Let us imagine, for example, a psychologist named Jones who, for scientific reasons, has adopted the hypothesis that human beings can best be described as complex electrical fields. This hypothesis, he thinks, has great explanatory value. He notes that friendship always involves complementary electrical phase patterns, just as hatred is correlated with conflicting phase patterns. Moreover, every feeling state can be correlated with readings on a certain instrument and thus be scientifically described in the categories of the second-order conceptual system. Because Jones holds this theory, he has decided that all concepts such as "consciousness," "the self," not to speak of "immortal soul," ought to be eliminated from the vocabulary. Jones, however, has a very deep friendship with Smith. He knows what it means to have an I-Thou relationship with Smith, to address him as "you," to have feelings of loyalty, obligation, guilt, and shame. His first-order discourse stays naturally within the language frame that makes use of the first and second person pronouns. He finds it quite appropriate on occasions to ask, "Can I count on you?" or to say, "Will you forgive me?" Jones is told that only the concept "soul" can "save these appearances." Jones does not believe this. He does not think the concept "soul" has any explanatory value at all. It has not proved useful in dealing with psychosomatic phenomena or schizophrenia or manic-depressive states or any other psychic phenomena with which he is concerned. In order to deal with these problems, Jones is driven to explore concepts that are parts of theories that involve appeals to different sorts of data and warrants. The arguments in this second-order discourse are technical and solicit a different kind of assent than is appropriate in first-order discourse which contains words like "I," "you," and the like. In short, Jones has learned to employ two different language frames, and the logical connections between them are not easy to discern. He experiences the same personal realities that others do who, for their part, employ the language of "the soul" or "the self," but he cannot accept their second-order explanatory language.

Now, consider the possibility that a cosmologist should someday establish the scientific utility of regarding the known universe as a great and complex electrical field. Just as in the case of human relationships where every feeling state can be correlated with certain scientific descriptions that are part of second-order theories about electrical fields, so too, here one will be able to correlate feelings of harmony with the universe with descriptions that function as parts of a larger explanatory hypothesis. One will then say that "cosmic consciousness" occurs when the wave patterns of a person (a microcosmic electrical field) are complementary to the wave patterns of the larger cosmic electrical field. The question is whether this second-order theory will in some way explain away or make inappropriate or false the first-order language and the behavior natural to it. Will anything change with respect to the concreteness of religious experience? There will presumably still be attitudes of awe, wonder, felt obligation, perhaps even prayer, that will seem appropriate to the religious person, a language that expresses the sense of presence. And will it not be possible to use this first-order language in certain contexts without assenting to any second-order, theory-laden concept such as "God" which functions as part of a metaphysical system?

There are at least two objections to this way of analyzing the matter. The first is to say that man cannot live satisfactorily with two such radically bifurcated language frames. Just as Kant's division between the pure and the practical reason demands a synthesis of some sort, so also does my division between the first-order language involving personal pronouns and second-order scientific language. Is it not the function of the metaphysician to provide this synthesis? Once again, I do not wish to put an a priori restriction upon the work of the metaphysician. He may wish to work away at providing just such a synthesis. I can only say that the alienated theologian does not now see much basis for hope that such a synthesis will be forthcoming. The fact is that with respect to our experience of other persons, we do use radically different kinds of language and conceptualities, the language of biochemical processes and the language in which pronouns such as "I" and "you" seem quite natural. Each language frame is rooted in a certain form of life which, in turn, directs our attention to certain qualities and relationships. At present, there seems to be no third schema that can mediate between these language frames. Therefore, the philosophical and theological problematic of the alienated theologian centers around the significance of this for religious discourse.

The other objection arises from the side of the unfriendly critic of religion. His intent is to attack the analogy I have drawn between the depth relationship between persons and the alleged religious I-Thou relationship. It is said that the analogy fails because we can identify and recognize persons and so specify when first-order discourse is appropriate. We cannot, however, recognize or identify God and, hence, specify when religious first-order discourse is appropriate. In short, we can fix the reference range of our first-order or even our second-order discourse about persons; we cannot do this in the case of the relationship to God.

This is, I believe, an important criticism and it requires much more attention than I can give it here. My answer would be along these lines: First of all, I am not at all sure that the mystic, at least, has the problem of identifying the kind of experience which invokes his first-order language. Indeed, the literature on the subject suggests that the experience is so unique as to be unmistakable even though its content is sometimes said to be ineffable. In the second place, the point of my analogy was to show that it is not necessary to employ the concept of "God" as a concept at all or to fix its reference range. Rather, what I wished to suggest was that there is an important logical difference between the question, Is there a Being, called God, who is experienced religiously and who is also the Cause of the world? and the question, Are there certain kinds of experiences the characteristics of which are such as to invoke naturally a language that has certain affinities with the language we use in depth relationships betwen persons? The first question can only be given an answer in the form of a hypothesis of some sort which will employ theory-laden conceptions that function as parts of a theory. The second question leads in a different direction, to the analysis of the expressions we use in certain unique relationships.[29] One can object to an explanatory hypothesis because it fails to explain, but how does one go about sustaining the objection to the mystic's use of "Thou"? One cannot say that there is no person to which he is referring because the mystic has not made the claim that there is. One cannot say the pronoun is inappropriate because this objection makes no sense. How can one legitimately object, for example, to e. e. cummings' use of the second person pronoun in the following lines of his poem beginning "i thank You God for most this amazing day"?

> how should tasting touching hearing seeing
> breathing any—lifted from the no
> of all nothing—human merely being
> doubt unimaginable You? [30]

Should we say that the "unimaginable You" has no reference range? But the poem fixes the kind of experience within which the pronoun naturally occurs, just as in the case of Wittgenstein's mysticism the name of God naturally arises in connection with the astonishment that anything exists, with the wonder at the order and intelligibility of the world, with the sense of being a part of the world as a whole and the affirmation of life that follows.

I can now imagine one of you responding to all of this by saying: "Well, you have come a long way, so long that I find it difficult to say that you are alienated at all. As a matter of fact, classical theism is consistent with much that you have said, unless, that is, you take all that business about the cosmic electrical field seriously. Why don't you accept theism as a 'likely story' (Plato) which has the merit of saving the phenomena?"

The answer is that the alienated theologian does not believe that classical theism is the best or the only likely story which saves the phenomena. The difficulty with theism is that it extrapolates from the religious experience in which the second person pronoun is natural to the existence of a personal being who has created the world and exercises a particular providence in it. The alienated theologian can accept the legitimacy of the first-order discourse, but he sees only a tenuous logical connection between this language and the theistic concept of God. At best, the alienated theologian's experience allows what Wittgenstein's piety allowed, a form of pantheism.[31] If the concept "God" is to be employed theoretically at all, then it seems to refer to an aspect of the world, a feature to which the human being can relate in a certain way and from which relationship certain attitudes and feelings follow. Because the alienated theologian is aware of the fundamental difference between himself at this point and traditional Christian belief, he cannot call himself a Christian theologian.

Why not, then, embrace process philosophy, for surely this metaphysical vision is more compatible with what I have said than classical theism? To this suggestion, the alienated theologian can only reply that in some respects it does seem more compatible. But his difficulty is that it is, nevertheless, a highly problematical hypothesis soliciting only the lightest assent and as such has all the difficulties as a vehicle for translating Christian belief that I have outlined above. Moreover, the alienated theologian cannot regard it as a faithful translation of the Christian belief in God, inextricably rooted as the latter is in the notion of causal efficacy. The process theologian is, in reality, also an alienated theologian except that for some reason he cannot accept the notion of being a straggler.

This, then, is my modest contribution to this consultation. I do not offer it as a program for the future of philosophical theology but merely as a description of the state of one of whom that might be said which was said of one of the characters in Anzengruber's play, *Die Dreuzelschreiber*, which had such an impact on Wittgenstein. In the play, this character tells how after a life of meaninglessness he experienced something like a religious revelation in which the problem of life no longer seemed like a problem. At the point of death, he had thrown himself down onto the long grass in the sunshine. He finally came to himself in the evening and experienced an unreasoning happiness, as though the sunshine had entered his body and he had been spoken to in the words: "Nothing can happen to you. . . . You're part of everything, and everything's part of you. Nothing can happen to you." Anton, another character in the play, then says to him: *"Du Sakra, du! Ja, was bist denn du nachher? Du bist ja kein Christ und kein Heid' und kein Turk'?!"* ("You are not a Christian, nor a pagan, nor a Turk.")[32]

NOTES

1. John B. Cobb, Jr., *God and the World* (The Westminster Press, 1969), p. 89.

2. See James F. Ross's review of Cobb's *God and the World* in the *Journal of the American Academy of Religion*, Vol. XXXVIII, No. 3 (Sept., 1970), pp. 310–315.

3. Paul Tillich, *The Shaking of the Foundations* (Charles Scribner's Sons, 1953), pp. 118–129.

4. Van A. Harvey, *The Historian and the Believer* (The Macmillan Company, 1966).

5. John Locke, *An Essay Concerning Human Understanding*, abr. and ed. by A. S. Pringle-Pattison (London: Oxford University Press, 1934), Book IV, Chapter XIX.

6. William K. Clifford, "The Ethics of Belief" in Walter Kaufmann (ed.), *Religion from Tolstoy to Camus* (Harper Torchbooks, 1961), p. 206.

7. G. M. Young, *Victorian Essays* (London: Oxford University Press, 1962), p. 7.

8. I do not mean to equate professional with logical fields, although there is often a close relationship. By a logical field I mean one in which the data and warrants are of one logical type. A professionalized field, such as history, may involve arguments in several logical fields. See my *Historian and the Believer*, Chapter II. I am indebted generally to the analysis of Stephen Toulmin, *The Uses of Argument* (Cambridge: Cambridge University Press, 1958).

9. Harvey, *ibid.*, Chapter IV.

10. Van A. Harvey and Schubert M. Ogden, "How New Is the "New Quest' of the Historical Jesus?" in Carl E. Braaten and Roy Harrisville (eds.), *The Historical Jesus and the Kerygmatic Christ* (Abingdon Press, 1964), pp. 197–242.

11. Harvey, *The Historian and the Believer*, Chapter V. Cf. my "Faith and Belief in Contemporary Theology," *Theology Today*, Vol. XVIII, No. 4 (1962), pp. 460–472.

12. See Langdon Gilkey, *Naming the Whirlwind: The Renewal of God-Language* (The Bobbs-Merrill Company, Inc., 1969).

13. See P. F. Strawson, *Individuals, An Essay in Descriptive Metaphysics* (Doubleday & Company, Inc., 1963), pp. xiii f. Cf. W. H. Walsh, *Metaphysics* (London: Hutchinson University Library, 1963), Chapter 3.

14. See R. I. Aaron, "Feeling Sure," *Proceedings of the Aristotelean Society*, Supp. Vol. XXX (1956), pp. 1–13.

15. Toulmin, *op. cit.*, p. 106.

16. Milton K. Munitz, *The Mystery of Existence* (Dell Publishing Company, Inc., 1968).

17. Van A. Harvey, "Is There an Ethics of Belief?" *The Journal of Religion*, Vol. LXIX, No. 1 (1969), pp. 41–58.

18. William James, "The Will to Believe," *Essays in Pragmatism* (Hafner Publishing Company, Inc. 1964), pp. 88–109.

19. Diogenes Allen, *The Reasonableness of Faith* (Corpus Books, 1969).

20. Unfortunately, I am unable to locate the precise reference.

21. See Munitz, *op. cit.*

22. See B. F. McGuinness, "The Mysticism of the *Tractatus*," *The Philosophical Review*, Vol. LXXV, No. 3 (July, 1966), pp. 305–328.

23. Loren Eiseley, *The Unexpected Universe* (Harcourt, Brace and World, Inc., 1969), p. 91.

24. William A. Christian, *Meaning and Truth in Religion* (Princeton University Press, 1964), Chapter VI.

25. William James, *The Varieties of Religious Experience* (The New American Library, Inc., 1958), p. 63.

26. McGuinness, "The Mysticism of the *Tractatus*," *loc. cit.*

27. See Julius Seelye Bixler, *Religion in the Philosophy of William James* (Marshall Jones Co., 1926), pp. 194 f.

28. W. T. Stace, *Mysticism and Philosophy* (London: Macmillan & Co., Ltd., 1961), pp. 71 ff.

29. On the dynamic function of naming, see Bernard Mayo, *The Logic of Personality* (London: Jonathan Cape, Ltd., 1952).

30. e. e. cummings, *Poems 1923–1954* (Harcourt, Brace and World, Inc., 1954), p. 464. Used by permission of the publishers, Harcourt, Brace Jovanovich, Inc.

31. See McGuinness, "The Mysticism of the *Tractatus*," *loc. cit.*, p. 321.

32. *Ibid.*, p. 328.

4

Philosophical Theology
as Confrontation*

HEINRICH OTT

In an essay entitled "Reason and Revelation" ("Vernunft und Offenbarung"), Theodor W. Adorno, the Frankfurt philosopher and sociologist who died recently, wrote against the modern "renaissance of the religion of revelation." He declared, "Were I able to accept the faith of revelation, that would involve attributing to it—over against my reason—an authority which would already presuppose that I have accepted it [faith] —an unavoidable circle." [1] He recommends a "most extreme asceticism over against every faith of revelation," [2] because this faith of revelation "would have to submit itself to the standard of objectivity, of knowledge . . . , whose claim it arrogantly dismisses." [3] Thus, Adorno sees only an absolute dichotomy between revelation and reason and believes that the conflict between them was already finally decided in the eighteenth century—to the disadvantage of the faith of revelation. This defeat was forgotten in the nineteenth century, however, and that accounts for the fact that in the twentieth century the faith of revelation together with its theology could once more have arisen as a strange apparition.

For us Christian theologians, this challenge is not new. Never-

---

* Translated by David Larrimore Holland, Professor of Church History, McCormick Theological Seminary.

theless, in the face of it, we cannot allow ourselves to rest with answers of the past, and the question is, How must we confront this challenge today? One might speak here of the immortality of the church established by Jesus Christ. But in this discussion it makes no sense to answer with an article of faith. It would be more appropriate to say: If the church of Christ is immortal, a continuous conversation between it and "reason" will always take place or at least will always be possible. The discussion may develop in various forms in different epochs, but the faith of revelation will never be able "arrogantly to dismiss" a legitimate claim by the demands of human knowledge. And, therefore, the appropriate answer to that verdict from the side of agnostics must consist in the concrete *question: How* indeed will the conversation between theology (and thus faith) on the one hand and what one somewhat summarily calls human "reason" on the other hand look, and how can this discussion remain a rational one, whose results can be expected to be plausible to anyone?

With that I have already come to my *thesis* with respect to "philosophical theology": philosophical theology will play an ever-expanding and decisive role in the future of the theological thought process; indeed, all theological thinking will gradually have to transform itself into philosophical theology. I want now first of all to define this thesis more precisely and then to argue for it.

On the definition: The thesis does not envision a transformation of the "theology of revelation" into "natural theology." Precisely for that reason we began with the dispute concerning the credibility of the faith *of revelation.* The revelation of God is that which should and will remain in constructive conversation with human reason—a conversation that may be arrogantly broken off neither from the side of reason nor from the side of the revelation faith. The theology of revelation (for instance in the sense of the dialectic theology of Karl Barth and Emil Brunner) thus will not disappear again in favor of a natural theology, but just this theology of revelation will articulate itself more and more as philosophical theology.

On the demonstration of the thesis: In the sense that theological thinking orients itself toward that upon which it can lean, the salvation-historical thought category today no longer provides a reliable platform. I say "thought *category*" quite consciously. It is not a matter here of the *content* of faith, but of the function of a category which was attributed to this content for a long time, of its function as a thought structure inside of which thought could go on. Concretely put, the "salvation-historical category" means the following: There is God and there is man. Between the two there is a *commercium*. Moreover, a history concerning both can be narrated which really has taken place, which takes place, and which will take place. Within the framework so constructed, then, the doctrines of creation and sin, Christology and soteriology, ecclesiology and eschatology—in short, all the traditional parts of the Christian dogmatics—are fitted in. Within this framework, for instance, the traditional theory of the crucifixion and atonement could be developed. Where this category dominated, the theology of revelation correctly saw its task to be literally to recapitulate the history and thereby to summarize the multiplicity of the Biblical sayings and to bring them to a simple, and the clearest possible, denominator. With this simplifying and collating recapitulation, helping terms which do not appear in Scripture itself become necessary from time to time. They are created, defined, and used by dogmatics within the salvation-historical context as instruments of the recapitulation. These are the specifically "theological" terms, as, for example, *causa secunda, unio hypostatica, regnum gratiae, ecclesia invisibilis,* etc.

This whole traditional procedure of theological reflection has become unbelievable today. The time of such a "Biblicistic dogmatics" is past. This style, this mode of expression of the dogmatic task, can no longer be retained. What has become unbelievable is not the recitation of the content of the faith (or as one says, the "saving facts" [*Heilstatsachen*]), as, for example, of the cross and the resurrection of Jesus Christ, but only that such matters are discussed within the salvation-historical scheme. As if this framework still stood firm as the self-evident ontological or preontological horizon within which every person moves and orients himself existentially! As if this *commercium* between God and man, in which something such as sin and atonement, justification and healing, etc., can for the first time take place, may be presupposed without further ado! This is by no means any longer self-evident! But the recapitulating Biblicistic dogmatics lives from precisely this vanished self-evidentness of a preontological salvation-historical horizon.

Incidentally, our critique of the recapitulating theology has an interesting philosophical parallel which perhaps will also prove henceforth to be meaningful. Martin Heidegger writes at the very beginning of *Sein und Zeit* concerning the method of his inquiry about Being: "The first philosophical step in understanding the problem of Being consists in not *muthon tina diēgeisthai*, in not 'telling a story,' i.e., in not defining entities as entities through regress to another entity in its origin, as if Being had the character of a possible entity. Being, as that which is asked about, thus demands its own mode of presentation which differs essentially from the discovery of entities." [4] I have no intention here of identifying the God-question of faith with the question of Being in Western philosophy. But the formal parallel is indeed striking, and it could be that there is here the beginning of a methodological relationship which we today must learn to follow, namely, that God too as the one questioned demands a "special mode of presentation."

Why is it no longer possible today, in philosophizing about the question of God, *muthon tina diēgeisthai?* Why has the salvation-historical framework become unbelievable? As a systematic theologian I decline to speculate very long concerning this question. Theology is not primarily the history of culture, and the evasion into historicizing (*historisieren*) and meta-historicizing (*meta-historisieren*) today often does a disservice with respect to the obligations of theological discourse. More-over, it would not be good if we were completely to unlearn the honest Scholastic *Sic et non*. The primary task of systematic theology is to discern the prevailing state of understanding and to orient itself to it, not to speculate concerning the reasons why it might have come to this state. (This last-mentioned sort of speculation, by the way, appears even less useful because apparently we are still less than clear ontologically concerning the essence of historical grounds or historical "causality" in general.)

If one attempts to explain the fact that the salvation-historical schema has become unbelievable by the thesis that "God is dead," one sets up only a sort of antisalvation history (*Anti-Heilsgeschichte*). A new story is told, a myth of the dying God, whose ontological outline is precisely as unclear and incompre-hensible as that of the traditional salvation-historical mythology and the Biblicistic dogmatics. Christian discourse in the twen-tieth century does not attain credibility by telling stories of a dead God instead of a living God.

At the conclusion of this initial argument let me say yet another word by way of terminological clarification: I have re-peatedly used the term "ontological" (*ontologisch*). Thus I spoke of the salvation-historical schema as an "ontological" or "preontological horizon" as speaking of a particular mode of talking about God and about divine things which belongs to the past. I understand "ontology" and "ontological," when I use these terms in intellectual theological discourse, not in the sense—which is at once general and specific—of Western metaphysics or of the general question of Being, but rather in the sense of that which Heidegger can occasionally call the regional ontologies, i.e., the ontologies of special regions of reality and of the knowledge of reality. One can raise questions everywhere either ontically, that is, concerning the relations of the individual real things to each other, or ontologically, that is, concerning the horizon within which these things appear and concerning the *modus* of their being real.

So our encounter with God in hearing and accepting the gospel is not just a matter of acquiring new ontic information. It carries with it implicitly a preontological understanding of what the reality, the *modus essendi* of God and of man before God, is. That is implicit, and it is the task of theological reflection to bring this implicit preontological understanding of this particular specific reality which encounters us to greater ontological clarity, to explicate the implicit.

Thus reflection follows life. *Lex orandi, lex credendi.* Reflexive discourse is by no means the first stage, but rather something lived, something existential to be thought of.

So far we have explained that the salvation-historical horizon in which theological discourse moved has become untenable and that a new style of theology has therefore become necessary. Theology—especially "theology of revelation," which derives from a revealing Word of God as a beginning and an opening— must articulate itself today as philosophical theology. What does that mean concretely? One can no longer speak of God in such a way that one tells stories about him (how he created the world, how he punishes the sinner, how he sent his Son to the earth, etc.)—as if the following were automatically comprehensible: (1) what it means (what we say by it when we say it) and (2) that it is true that such stories happen. But how should one *then* speak of God (of the self-revealing, speaking, acting God!)?

We must withdraw the "salvation events" from the salvation-historical framework where one can still recite them simply as facts, and transpose them (*über-setzen*). This transposition (*Über-setzung*) I have always called an "existential interpretation"; hence we can say: existential interpretation is the consistent articulation of the theology of revelation as philosophical theology. In this I consciously speak of the events of salvation in the plural in order to make clear that—like my teacher Rudolf Bultmann—I intend no reductionism. Rather, all the facts of salvation, as they are summarized, for instance, in the Apostles' Creed, must be articulated philosophically in the specific content of their meaning. In fact they must be articulated philosophically *as event*, i.e., not as "natural" givens of the human existence in general, but as something that always approaches man from without and creates for him a new situation.

But now if we have come this far together, what does it mean "to articulate philosophically"? It means to unfold the content of the faith in the same terms with which a philosophical mind also contemplates the reality of man and of his world. This is the way in which revelation faith and "human reason" can remain in a constructive conversation! Faith, to begin with, must not use another language and employ other terms. It should express itself in the same terms and in the same style of ideas as the philosopher. Thus it should become plain that it has something real and relevant to say. That it has something radically new to say over against all human consciousness and that this new wine splits open the old wineskins and ruptures the old terms must then be proved. And this will appear when theological thinking, with rigorous (not arbitrary and eclectic) use of philosophical terms, arrives at the point where, in order to remain true to its task, it must modify and recast the terms. Faith may not be allowed, in doctrinaire fashion, to start by placing itself at a point outside of all philosophic conceptuality. The new beginning, the break of the "natural" continuity by means of the gospel, must, so to speak, be made visible within the philosophical conceptuality itself. Whoever resists this requirement in order simply to tell a holy story adopts from the outset a sacral area outside all philosophical reflection concerning man and his world. He has in fact arrogantly rejected the legitimate claim of human ration-

ality! From his Archimedean point he then uses special philosophical terms arbitrarily and eclectically as tools, as, in a certain sense, disposable articles.

The salvation-historical schema assures theology a sacral zone
inside the world. This sacral zone is under attack today. Here,
indeed, the principle of secularization is valid! The articulation
of the theology of revelation as philosophical theology on the
other hand perpetuates the incarnation of the Word of God
into flesh, into human history, and also in the realm of thought.

At this point now I can finally try to define our main term,
"philosophical theology." Before these considerations that
would not have been possible. This term, as you know, is
seldom encountered in Europe, at least not in the technical
sense of designating a particular discipline at centers of theological education. Roman Catholics know "fundamental theology"
as a discipline. Karl Rahner, differing from traditional fundamental theology, develops the concept of a "formal and
fundamental theology," which he delineates as "that part of
strictly systematic theology which elaborates the 'formal' and
permanent basic structures of the salvation-history (the basic
relationship of God and creation; the concept of personal revelation of deed and word in general; the concept of redemptive
revelation)." [5] And Rahner adds: this theology is " 'fundamental' insofar as it confronts this general and formal pattern of
the Christian revelation with the formal structures of the human
intellectual life in general within which, after all, this history
of revelation takes place, into which it plunges itself and from
which some approach to it [this historical revelation] must be
established." [6]

This specification of the term comes closest to what we
want to understand here under "philosophical theology"—
except that Karl Rahner uses the term "salvation history" differently from the way we have been using it just now. We meant
by the "salvation-historical schema" that protected sacral area
inside of which—in a certain sense without problems and

unencumbered by all philosophical problematic—stories can be told about God and man. In contrast to that, Rahner's (and, in general, modern Roman Catholicism's) concept of "salvation history" means the revelation event (which is at the same time the event of redemption) which, coming from God, encounters man in his situation and reshapes that situation.

In order to simplify matters, let us speak more specifically of the Protestant and of the Catholic definitions of the term "salvation history." In the Protestant definition the accent lies on the linear course of the events. With the Catholic definition it lies on the real encounter of the divine revelation with human reality, with the "human intellectual life." With the Protestant definition the philosophical question is obfuscated in the sense that it is presupposed as self-evident that such events have taken place and that one can recapitulate them. With the Catholic definition, on the other hand, precisely the philosophical question moves into the burning point of theological interest in that it must be shown and articulated how the real encounter between the divine revelation and the "human intellectual life," into which it plunges itself, works itself out in the latter.

For that reason, Rahner emphasizes strongly the confrontation (and for my part I want to add: the interlocking) of the structures of revelation on the one hand and of the structures of the human intellectual life on the other. And on this point now, in my judgment, the whole effort of theological thinking must concentrate both today and in the future: on the confrontation, on the interlocking. What the revelation of God is, what really takes place in it, and what it means must be expressed in terms of the human intellectual life. But what the "human intellectual life" (to retain Rahner's expression here) is, must in turn be interpreted in the light of revelation. Neither side may claim a methodological primacy. Everything depends on the confrontation. The effort that must take place here in order to embrace this confrontation is at once a theological and a philosophical one. For that reason, the term "philosophical theology" is appropriate.

At the end of this train of thought I can now *repeat and specify more precisely the thesis* which I set forward at the outset of the lecture: Proceeding from the Word of God, I am doing theology of revelation. But the salvation-historical theology of revelation today must abdicate in favor of a philosophical theology of revelation. And that means: instead of telling *stories* about God and man, theology must reflect upon how the *event* of the divine revelation works itself out among men.

Let me say at this point that I see no difficulties in starting as a theologian of revelation, in taking the fact of divine revelation witnessed in the Scriptures as my starting point.

There is always a primordial datum which sets the process of reflective thought into motion. "The symbol gives rise to thought," says Paul Ricoeur. There must be something that gives us something to think about, some primal content of a yet unarticulated, unthought meaning, as, for instance, if we read a poem or regard a work of art. This can be explicated subsequently, and thus its relevance may be revealed by rational discourse to those who do not yet understand its meaning, its "relevance," that is, what new aspects of meaning it may convey, what new elucidation or illumination it may bring to their own being. Therefore, I feel very sympathetic indeed to David Burrell's parallelism of theology and literary criticism.

To carry the train of thought farther I want to set down at this point *two decisions* respecting the path of thinking. I wish to force these upon nobody, but I can and must establish and account for the path I have chosen:

1. The first decision relates to the point of departure: I believe that in our theological-philosophical effort we have to depart from that reality and that experience which I want to label "primary reality" (*Primärwirklichkeit*) and "primary experience (*Primärerfahrung*), and I, in any case, want to commit

myself to this path. In connection with Rahner we spoke of
the "human intellectual life" into which the divine revelation
plunges itself. I myself spoke earlier of the "reality of man and
of his world." Both terms specify the same thing, namely,
precisely the place where theological and philosophical reflection of necessity encounter each other. The question becomes:
How does this reality make itself accessible to us? From whence
and under what viewpoint does the philosophical (and then
also the theological) approach to it ensue? Here, it seems to
me, we must hold fast to that which for every man, for us
all, is primary, to the primary human mode of access to reality.
But this is that way of experiencing which each of us as a
person originally makes: in his being with other persons, in his
being alone with himself, in his being in the midst of men,
animals, and things, which he can perceive and touch with the
organs of his body. Certainly this experience is "subjectively"
stamped. But it is not on that account uncommunicable. No
absolute barriers exist between subjects: there is rather a solidarity of experiencing which proves itself time after time. Communication concerning primary experiences which are subjectively molded also has its own mode of rationality. And here too
it is finally a matter of truth and not simply of subjective im-
pressions. Moreover, this area of primary experience is not, as
with a narrow empiricism, restricted to the data of the senses,
but it comprehends no less, and actually, it comprehends above
all the "inner" experiences of feeling, willing, thinking, hoping,
etc.

Now, through these primary experiences, the reality of man
and of his world is not only more primordially, but also more
essentially, accessible than through an "objective," statistical
stock-taking of the data yielded. The statistical mode of understanding is dependent on primary experience. So, e.g., a statistical poll concerning the occurrence of a particular sort of
human behavior in society can only be understood, only then
does it "say something," if one understands the primary ex-

perience, at least in its contours, which ordinarily corresponds to the behavior in question. Thus *statistical identification*, which only knows the "facts of the case," is rooted in *hermeneutical understanding*, which is oriented to the category of the meaning of the comprehensible personal experience. On this basis, the hermeneutical understanding of human phenomena is that area of philosophical reflection which is relevant for a philosophical theology.

Here I would like to argue with Mr. Jones, the psychiatrist in Van Harvey's magnificent paper, the man who regards all human beings as complex electrical fields.[7] In my opinion, Mr. Jones, if he has experienced true friendship and an I-Thou relationship with his friend Smith, is simply inconsistent: He knows, he has experienced (as we all have), the reality of the personal, and thus he must be aware that this cannot be matched by any explanatory talk about electrical fields. This reality demands or gives way to reflective talk, but reflective talk of quite another type. It seems to me that Wittgenstein, in his *Lectures and Conversations on Aesthetics, Psychology and Religious Belief*, makes a strong case for this rejection of explanatory, causalistic psychology. If we truly follow along this line, then, there might be a valuable option to be found for the "alienated theologian" which, in a certain sense, is what we all are.

2. The second decision regards the procedure: it is the decision to *abandon a system* (*Systemverzicht*). Karl Rahner wants to confront the general formal structures of human intellectual life and the formal structures of the history of revelation. But which past, present, or future philosopher can provide us with the appropriate synoptic view of the structures of human intellectual life? Are we not to be able even to begin with the work of philosophical theology before this difficult question is decided? Indeed, all of our discussions during this conference have seemed to me to reveal a great embarrassment among us theologians with regard to the puzzling pluralism of philosophical options. Or must we, perhaps without sufficient

grounds, decide at the outset for a particular system as a tool
to work with? I think we can and should go to our work even
without a systematic synopsis of the reality of man and of
his world. Corresponding to the multiplicity of the aspects of
the divine revelation and of the multiplicity of the aspects of
human reality, the confrontation must be accomplished in
manifold ways, and we cannot wait for a systematic synopsis.
Every aspect of revelation demands, in order to be unfolded,
confrontation and philosophic articulation. And every aspect of
human reality demands, in the last analysis, a theological interpretation.

Here I should like to comment briefly on the papers of
Schubert Ogden and David Burrell. Schubert Ogden wants to
establish theology in a system of fundamental anthropological,
cosmological, and philosophico-theological insights. I am skeptical with regard to such totality systems, and I am not willing
to wait until somebody succeeds in convincing me entirely.
Therefore, I feel closer to David Burrell's model of theology as
"literary criticism," as starting with the "particular poem," so
to speak, of divine revelation in Christ. We must, as theologians,
climb to the particular, to the specific, trying to interpret it in
the light of the end, as long as we live, to relate it to every
experience that occurs in our horizon.

Nevertheless, in some respects I feel close to Schubert Ogden
too. For in the process of interpreting the particular we find
ourselves placed face to face with basic, undeniable, unjustifi-
able facts, such as man's self-awareness or his awareness of
another person. We have to account for these facts, these basic
phenomena or structures. We have to take them into our
discourse for interpretation, and they will prove to be indispensable and helpful, truly illuminating means within the
process of interpretation.

This abandonment of system is, of course, neither doctrinaire
nor a matter of absolute principle. Perhaps from the many

tesserae of the mosaic of the confrontation someday a greater vision will emerge.

It now remains to illustrate with a few examples how this philosophical theology, understood as an always particular confrontation (*Einzel-Konfrontation*) of divine revelation and human reality, may work. I want to indicate at least four problem areas. In the first two cases a philosophical problem poses itself in the area of the hermeneutical primary realities. In each case the problem has not yet been finally thought through and with each a confrontation with revelation could prove itself to be fruitful for further philosophical thought as well as for theology (as a new possibility of articulating revelation). In the subsequent two cases we shall deal with special problems of dogmatics which emerge with the unfolding of the witness of the divine revelation and which, for the sake of the clarity of the development, are in need of a philosophical articulation.

1. The first problem concerns the essence of *language*. Ludwig Wittgenstein, in his *Lectures and Conversations on Aesthetics, Psychology and Religious Belief* [8] (which were taken down by his students), has struggled to grasp what takes place in discourse concerning religious things. So far as I can see, he did not reach any conclusion. The following sentences from the first lecture on religious faith give us evidence of this struggle.

"Why shouldn't one form of life culminate in an utterance of belief in a Last Judgment? But I couldn't answer either 'Yes' or 'No' to the statement that there will be such a thing. Nor 'Perhaps,' nor even 'I'm not sure.'—It is a statement which may not allow of any such answer. . . . If an atheist says: 'There won't be a Judgment Day, and another person says there will,' [sic] do they mean the same?—Not clear what criterion of meaning the same is." (sic) [9]

Wittgenstein struggles to understand the religious language

game and the religious form of life and experience of reality
out of which the former grows. Thus for Wittgenstein everything is open: his sentences express, first of all, the truly
original philosophical astonishment in the face of the phenomenon, and the initial questioning, which first brings to
consciousness the fact that the problems are open, and which
therefore breaks through the self-evident aspects of the average
normal comprehension. (For as average Christians or atheists
we are at first indeed inclined to regard it as a matter of course
that one can answer the question about the Last Judgment
with "Yes" or "No" or "I am not sure.") As a theologian I
am taken aback by the question of the philosopher and at the
moment I do not want to go a single step farther in dis-
seminating premature answers, but rather, I want to let the
question simply stand as a challenge to our usual self-under-
standings. But if in the future we have to think further about
the problem, it may be expedient for us to observe that Wittgenstein's lectures concerning religious faith belong, both in
time and in subject matter, in consort with his lectures on
aesthetics. (Both were held in the summer of 1938.) This
association may assist us in pondering the question posed for
us theologians, and many ideas to which the lectures on aesthetics give us access may subsequently be transferable into
the field of the religious language problems which Wittgenstein
has set up.

Wittgenstein's lectures on aesthetics seem to me to be one
single struggle to overcome a positivistic understanding of language and of reality. Aesthetic experience and aesthetic judgment, even in their most trivial form (Wittgenstein, like Heidegger, likes to illustrate his points from everyday and trivial
phenomena), are reestablished in their own right. The aes-
thetical cannot be grasped through causal explanation—and
even if one attempts it, it is not thereby understood as the
aesthetic. "There is a 'Why?' to aesthetic discomfort, not a
'cause' to it." [10] His linguistic acuity always led Wittgenstein

to influence the establishment of goals, even the establishment of values with a view to the society of the future.

This philosophical clarification and deepening, which amounts really to winning a philosophical horizon in general, will have to go in the *hermeneutical* direction. This means that the social data are not, like the physical data, natural, even though one can apprehend them statistically and can draw conclusions from this apprehension. Society consists of men, and even the statistically assessable average behavior of men in society, in their social roles, is constituted originally out of comprehensible personal decisions: decisions in which man is authentically himself, and decisions in which he is inauthentic and lost within what Heidegger calls "People" ("*das Man*")—but decisions nevertheless. Even "deficient," incomplete decisions (and these may be in the majority), by which man is predominantly determined from the outside, still remain understandable decisions. The personal character is not fully lost, and though human behavior may indeed be comparable with instinctive animalic behavior—it is not essentially identifiable with it. That is, man is not a person acting understandably *in addition* to his being a social entity, but precisely *as* a social entity, in his averageness, he is a person. For that reason, we need a *hermeneutics of society*. This will go hand in hand with the empirical investigation of social realities and must always remain connected to it. It will have to teach us really to *understand* the results of these realities as human phenomena. What emerges as understandable in the constellation of a group? What actually happens if a new social trend appears? If, for example, among theologians a new school or trend develops or disappears again? That is the sort of question which one must pose here. The theological implications of this philosophical posing of the problem for ecclesiology and ethics are obvious.

Let me give an additional hint here too: I suppose that (among other things) what we would have to do would be to investigate the relationship and interaction between an authentically and an inauthentically existential grasp of the same meaning, of the same meaningful attitude or behavior. For a collective mode of behavior is on the average inauthentic, lost in "*das Man*" ("People"). (According to Heidegger, behavior within the mode of "*das Man*" can be thoroughly vital and morally good.) Patterns of collective behavior are for instance disseminated by way of imitation. Imitation is mostly an inauthentic type of existential attitude. Nevertheless, it is a meaningful, understandable act. What is the "hermeneutics of the inauthentic"? What is actually going on here?

3. My third paradigmatic problem relates itself to the *interim situation of the dead* between their death and the Last Judgment. This appears to be a very traditional and dogmatic question, and a liberally inclined Protestantism has regarded itself as long since emancipated from such questions as pure mythology. But today we stand in a worldwide discussion with our Roman Catholic colleagues who are obligated by the magisterium and tradition to raise such questions. And who knows? Perhaps we are dealing here not simply with an outworn mythology; perhaps the ecumenical dialogue, which brings with it solidarity in working through such questions, may contribute to the expansion and greater philosophical differentiation of the horizons of our problems.

In this particular case the question of the *essence of time* must be posed. Are the dead at the point of the Last Judgment simultaneously with their death, as Emil Brunner taught? Do they therewith at the moment of death just drop out of time? And what would it mean, then, that time borders in such a fashion on eternity, indeed empties into eternity? Can a concept of time be articulated philosophically which contains this possibility? The dogmatic question requires the rigors of philosophical thought!

Here my hint and suggestion would be that we might further examine the three time dimensions, namely, past, present, and future, in their interpretation, their perichoresis.[15] Time, in which we as persons exist, is neither simply linear, nor cyclical, nor punctiliar. These are insufficient notions. But the time dimensions lock into each other. In this interpenetration of our historical time, is there an element of eternity, of a final, eschatological confrontation? Would such a notion make sense with regard to our lived time, which we experience every day? Could there be a confrontation with eternity in every moment, a hidden presence of eternity in the midst of the time we live? If so, we could better understand what death means.

These are presentiments, not more, and, as such, anything but clear. But it is my opinion that our thinking is always guided by presentiments and that only by passing through the zone of presentiment can we reach clarity about every existentially important subject matter.

4. The fourth problem concerns the *salvific meaning of Christ's cross*. If the cross of Christ has a salvific meaning for man which surpasses simply an imitative model, then in the cross a solidarity with man in his innermost self has obviously become event. This event must be articulated philosophically, for otherwise the story of the cross as the reconciling deed of God remains just an incredible salvation-historical "story." But that means that a concept of personhood has to be conceived according to which, in the innermost essence of a person, such a solidarity is conceivable.

Finally, I want to come back once more to the observation that the abandonment of a system of philosophical theology may not be doctrinaire, fundamental, and final. In reflecting on the innumerable individual problems that do present and will present themselves to us, perhaps a convergence will emerge into a comprehensive theological-philosophical anthropology. This could be a *dialogical* anthropology which is not dominated by a general notion of "human nature" or a general a priori of human perception, feeling, and willing, but which also is not

simply content with the individual results of positive anthropological research. For this sort of anthropology, rather, the
event of communication stands in the center as that which is
really human. The event of communication, even between distant and separated worlds, is that which is not predictable on
the basis of a general anthropological a priori, but rather, simply
eventuates. It is that toward which we again and again con-
fidently look and move ahead, because it occurs in that uncontrollable continuum of the presence of God, in which we "live
and move and have our being."

Let me give here a final additional hint. I doubt whether we
have an a priori principle ready at hand to explain how communication can possibly happen. And nevertheless it happens
again and again. People understand each other.

Is it not a curious fact, to give an example, that we are all
convinced that there is no human language which in principle
we would not be able to learn if we would live together with the
people who speak this language? This conviction that communication *would* be possible is almost as strong as our self-
awareness of the "I" or as our awareness of the "Thou."

Or let me mention one of my favorite texts: Heidegger's
dialogue with the Japanese in *Unterwegs zur Sprache*.[16] Through
many difficulties these partners come to be able to communicate
about what they mean by "language." They feel that they communicate. And they can explain what they mean. This language
game might first be valid only for the two of them. But then a
third one, a fourth one, and so on might enter. They will explain to him. Thereby they will enlarge their language game,
taking into account the experiences and the life horizons of
these new people.

There is no irrationalism in this idea, because one can explain, make plausible, communicate what he experiences, and
thus he will reach new people and make them understand.

But we can't dispose of the event of communication in advance. There is no instrumental a priori principle that we can

handle. Communication is always full of surprises. But it happens.

That it happens might have to do with every man's being confronted with God, whether he knows it or not. There might, so to speak, be a "proof of God," not "e consensu gentium," as earlier theologians put it, but "e communicatione gentium."

That is just another presentiment, of course. But I have already told you what I think about presentiment and thought. So let's try to go ahead doing philosophical theology! Let us try! This dialogical anthropology is, however, perhaps still a distant vision toward which precisely we, in the age of the planetary units of mankind and in the age of a new confrontation among the world religions, are just beginning to advance.

NOTES

1. Theodor W. Adorn, "Vernunft und Offenbarung," *Stichworte* (Frankfurt, 1969), pp. 25 f.
2. *Ibid.*, p. 28.
3. *Ibid.*, p. 26.
4. Martin Heidegger, *Sein und Zeit* (Tübingen: Max Niemeyer Verlag, 1949), Art I, § 2.
5. Karl Rahner, "Formale und fundamentale Theologie," in Karl Rahner and H. Vorgrimler (eds.), *Kleines theologisches Wörterbuch* (Freiburg im Breisgau: Herder & Co., 1961).
6. *Ibid.*
7. See Harvey, above, p. 136.
8. Ludwig Wittgenstein, *Lectures and Conversations on Aesthetics, Psychology, and Religious Belief*, ed. by Cyril Barrett (University of California Press, 1966).
9. *Ibid.*, Lecture I, p. 58.
10. *Ibid.*, Lecture II, § 19, p. 14.
11. *Ibid.*, Lecture IV, § 4, p. 31.
12. *Ibid.*, Lecture II, § 5, p. 12.
13. *Ibid.*, Lecture III, § 1, p. 19.
14. Martin Heidegger, "Aletheia," *Vorträge und Aufsätze* (Pfullingen: Neske Verlag, 1954), p. 258.

15. Cf., for instance, Heidegger's recent essay, "Zeit und Sein," 1968, or my analysis of the theme in my book, *Der persönliche Gott* (Göttingen: Vandenhoeck & Ruprecht, 1969).

16. Martin Heidegger, *Unterwegs zur Sprache* (Pfullingen: Neske Verlag, 1959).

5

Dialogue on the Future
of Philosophical Theology: A Report
DONALD M. MATHERS

1. EXPERIENCE AS A BASIS
FOR PHILOSOPHICAL THEOLOGY

Michael Novak began the first discussion with the remark that all the papers presented to the Consultation placed great weight on human experiences as a starting point and as a source of evidence for philosophical theology. In the case of Schubert Ogden's paper, this starting point is described as the "common faith" of man, "the basic existential faith which is constitutive of human existence," "the faith that grounds and encompasses the whole of our human life and thought," "the faith by which every man exists simply as a man." Ogden gives two examples of this common faith, first the basic faith which is tacitly presupposed by the whole enterprise of scientific explanation— the faith, namely, that the world of events of which we believe ourselves to be parts is so ordered that our experience of phenomena in the past and the present warrants our having certain expectations of the future. The second example is the basic faith underlying all our moral behavior and language that some course of action open to us ought to be followed and that it ought to be a course which, so far as possible, includes the realization rather than the frustration of the various vital interests affected by our action.

Much of the discussion in the first session centered on the plausibility of Ogden's description of this common faith of man, and a variety of objections to it were offered—the fact that men exhibit varying degrees of trust and distrust toward their environment, the possibility that there might be a false or inauthentic faith, the charge that Ogden was too quick to interpret men's confidence and trust in religious terms, the likelihood that men's basic attitudes to the world were more complex than was suggested by Ogden's description.

On the first point, Donald Evans argued that if the starting point of philosophical theology is to be described in terms of faith as confidence toward one's environment, then one had better reckon with the fact that there are great variations in this confidence. At one end of the scale there is unconditional and total confidence, but more commonly men exhibit a varied trust and mistrust, while at the other end of the scale (which would no doubt be a kind of mental illness) they totally mistrust their world. If we are to make the common faith of man our starting point, we cannot describe it as unconditional trust, but only as that minimal trust without which we cannot live a sane life.

In a similar vein, David Burrell argued that words such as "trust" hardly described the existential path of man. My trust, he said, is flawed and faulted and shot through with mistrust. And Michael Novak commented that Alfred North Whitehead (on whom Ogden relies so heavily) makes more sense in the Midwest than anywhere else in the world. He missed in Ogden a sense of the negativities—things are much stickier than you would suppose from reading Whitehead. Charles Scott argued that alongside animal faith there is also animal distrust, and if philosophical theology were to investigate one, it had better investigate the other, although this would make the starting point more ambiguous and the move to classical metaphysics more difficult.

Ogden's reply was that he was more than willing to recognize the negativities in life and saw the value of an argument like that in Langdon Gilkey's *Naming the Whirlwind.* But the basic question is the relation of the negative and the positive. What is lack of confidence? Is it possible to talk of a total lack of trust? Could anyone live in total mistrust? No doubt the religious question does rise in negative terms for many people, but to put the positive and the negative on the same level would make it impossible to make sense of traditional metaphysics and theology. There must be a positive core to all negative reactions. He had tried, for instance, to study suicide, and what struck him was that the negativities involved always seemed to have a positive ground. He thought that Albert Camus gave support to this—Camus had repudiated the title of prophet of despair as being a contradiction in terms, and had said that to talk of a literature of despair was meaningless.

Van Harvey pointed to a sentence in Ogden's paper which raised a somewhat different point—not lack of faith, but false or inauthentic faith. "Even a false or inauthentic faith," Ogden had written, "which we sometimes speak of as 'unfaith,' is not simply the absence of faith but faith itself in its negative mode." Does this mean that alongside the "common faith" of man there could be a primary inauthentic faith?

Ogden replied by quoting a distinction of Frederick Ferré's between the intensive dimension of faith and that dimension of faith which has to do with the object. All faith as intensive is a matter of concern or trust, and this is true whether the faith is authentic or inauthentic. Authentic and inauthentic have to do with the mode of faith. True and false are related to the object of faith. Authentic faith means sincere trust, inauthentic means conditional trust; so it is possible to have inauthentic faith in a true object and authentic faith in a false object. As an example of inauthentic faith, he quoted Luther's exegesis of the First Commandment in his Large Catechism. Faith and God are inseparably connected; when you know where men look for their final succor, you know what is their god. It might be money or power, and while this probably should not be interpreted as meaning that men worship their pocketbooks directly, there are people whose pocketbooks are a condition of their trust in God. Inauthentic faith in God means a faith in God conditional on something else. The mode of faith and the object of faith cannot be separated any more than the distinction authentic/inauthentic and the distinction true/false.

Frederick Sontag drew attention to a statement in Ogden's paper that religion in its varying expressions is the primary and most direct reflection of the basic existential faith by which we all live simply as men. He felt that this showed a theologian's bias; it made religion too universal. If the statement were true, then everyone must either be natively religious or be unreflective. But it is becoming obvious that nowadays practically a majority of men live without a religious sensitivity. Theology is still possible in this situation but it can hardly be continuous with universal human experience.

Ogden's reply was that he did not find it so obvious that men are irreligious, if religion is taken in the broad sense of trust and its possibilities. Indeed, he thought it patently obvious that men are religious—their ultimate concern is evident even if it is not expressed in institutional religion. The irreligiousness of contemporary men is due to a lack of options of meaningful religious symbols.

To this, Sontag responded that even if this were granted, Ogden moves too easily from ultimate concern to formal religion. Men may have a basic faith, but they cannot easily move to a more technical one.

Much later in the Consultation, Donald Evans raised two points that are relevant to the question of experience as a basis for philosophical theology. He felt prepared to defend the possibility of philosophical theology as reflection on religious language, since attitudes imply ontologies, but he saw a problem in the plurality of starting points. For example, mystical experience, wonder, and a sense of the numinous are all real forms of religious experience and all spoke to something in him, but he could lay no claim to universality for any of them, and that put him in a very different position from Schleiermacher, who had only one starting point in religious experience.

Evans' second problem was, How do you move from the description of experience to the development of philosophical theology? If you start with the examination of elusive human attitudes such as trust and gratitude and reflect on them, you do seem to be committing yourself to "something out there," as Cook Wilson and John Baillie did when they argued from their own sense of gratitude to the existence of a personal Being to whom they were grateful. But this can be done in two ways: (1) reflection on a state of consciousness and an elusive reference to what is implied in it, or (2) Ogden's method of trying to conceive and to spell out what it is that is implied.

Ogden admitted this was a real difficulty, but he did not think that the two ways were in the end mutually exclusive. Michael Novak agreed and felt that Evans had posed the difference too sharply—there is a middle position between wonder and concept which is critical for theology. This problem became central in the discussion of David Burrell's paper and tended to focus on the question whether metaphysics is constructive or analytic.

2. METAPHYSICS, CONSTRUCTIVE OR ANALYTIC?

The feature of David Burrell's paper on which the second discussion tended to focus was his characterization of metaphysics as analytic in contrast to Schubert Ogden's more traditional view of metaphysics as constructive. Burrell saw the older style of metaphysics as the attempt to speak directly about the world as a transempirical object, "to say something about everything," as explanation proceeding by way of general theory, or even as a lusting after an authoritative system. By contrast, he saw the newer style as critical endeavor, as elucidating the logical features of a situation, a path to enlightenment rather than an attempt at explanation, an exercise in using what language we have in such a way as to call attention to the manner in which we are using it, as conceptual therapy.

Jerry Gill had noted this contrast when he commented that Ogden's paper was very metaphysical in the old sense. Instead of simply pointing to what was tacitly presupposed and then remaining silent, it had sought to conceptualize it. Ogden had questioned the distinction when he replied with the question, "How do you know when to quit? If you are to identify the tacit presupposition, how can you do so except by discursive talk?"

Thomas Ogletree described the contrast by saying that Burrell wanted to remind us that you couldn't conceptualize God, and to emphasize not general theory about reality but logical forms. Ogden, on the other hand, wanted to speak of God in terms of constructive metaphysics.

The Consultation was pretty evenly divided between these two views—Burrell was accused of vagueness and imprecision and Ogden of monolithic rigidity. Not surprisingly, there was no resolution of the problem, though its shape became clearer, and there was a better understanding of the issues involved.

We will begin with Ogden's position, where the issues were more clear-cut. In a variety of ways people argued that it failed to take account of the pluralism in the present philosophical and theological position. John Burkhart asked how seriously Ogden took the plurality of positions that confronted the philosophical theologian and asked whether, given this plurality, "philosophy" could hope to function as a prolegomenon to theology. Joseph Bracken argued that we should be grateful for the plurality of philosophies, for if we had only one philosophy and many theologies, that would give an undue priority to philosophy, and theology would be cramped and limited by having only one exclusive philosophical frame of reference available to it. For example, Aristotelian Thomism and Kant's *Religion Within the Bounds of Reason Alone* both presupposed a single philosophical framework which alone was supposed capable of giving intelligibility to religion. Michael Novak felt not only that Ogden's paper implied a single metaphysic conceived as a science but that it also implied a single denominational theology and failed to recognize that in religious studies today you have to be more pluralistic. It was even suggested by Thomas Parker that Ogden's system was imperialistic: one philosophy, one theology, one religion.

Ogden's reply to these criticisms was to say that the philosopher must indeed begin with his own situation, in our case a highly pluralistic one, but his goal is to transcend this historical starting point. He takes it as a datum in order to explore its implications. Just as the theologian begins with the conviction that universal truth is disclosed in this place and in this time, so the philosopher must try to abstract from the historical situation in which he begins. Short of the *eschaton* we will always have to live with pluralism, and it is good that there should be many forms of theistic metaphysics, but there is not a plurality of equally adequate positions, and one must always drive for the exclusion of the relatively less adequate for the sake of the truth. Both in science and in religion there is both plurality and unity, and when Ogden used the word "science" in his paper as a possible description of philosophy, he put it in quotation marks, meaning simply creative reflection pressing for clarity and seeking to avoid the extremes of vagueness and incoherence. As to the examples of Kant and Thomas, he saw a significant difference. Kant was more self-conscious about the primacy of philosophy and wore it as a badge of honor, playing down revealed religion. For Thomas, on the other hand, theology is always a negative norm vis-à-vis philosophy.

The discussion of Burrell's approach to metaphysics focused on his three claims that theology was like grammar, that the

skills of the theologian are analogous to those employed by the
literary critic, and that the criteria which the theologian employs
in his work are displayed but cannot be articulated.

Frederick Sontag questioned the appropriateness of compar-
ing theology to grammar, and pointed out that the analogy broke
down in the case of God. Burrell comes to the rather mystical
conclusion that there is little or nothing that we can say directly
about God. If this is true, then God is the exception to most of
the rules, and one wonders what value is left in the view that
theology is grammar if it cannot cover the central case of God.

Dallas High had a different worry. He had counted at least
seven metaphors in Burrell's paper which attempted to explain
what could be meant by the word "grammar" in this specialized
Wittgensteinian sense. He was uncomfortable about this and
wondered whether it led to elucidation or confusion. "Should
I trade in a set of rigorous explanations that may be monolithic
for a set that may be equivocal? Should I run the risk of making
a method out of equivocation?"

Frederick Ferré wondered whether Burrell's position was
really an analytic one at all. He suspected it was really some kind
of Zen Christianity where koans are proposed for which there
is no solution but which are meant to help us see that the truth
is inexpressible.

On the second issue, the analogy between theology and
literary criticism, Burrell got much stronger support, for instance from Heinrich Ott, who said he liked the model. But it
was Ian Barbour who suggested that the analogy of literary
criticism might do something to provide a middle ground between the idea of theology as explanation (on the model of
science) and negative theology (which stresses the impossibility
of describing or explaining God and laid the emphasis on the
noncognitive functions of language). The analogy of literary
criticism points not only to the inadequacy of language but also
to the appropriateness of language, and thus brings Burrell
somewhat closer to Ogden.

Michael Novak seemed to give some support to this when he said, on the one hand, that there was a kind of relativism built into what Burrell was doing, but on the other, that literary criticism does require you to become more aware of the implicit values involved, and that great literary critics become like philosophers or theologians. It comes down to testimony, the willingness to enter into argument.

On his third point, that the criteria which a theologian employs in his work can be displayed but cannot be articulated, Burrell got both support and opposition. Ott and Novak both urged the need to recognize the place of mystery in theology. I am not shocked, said Ott, at the idea of a pregiven mystery. There are primary facts which need no justification. And Novak commented that anyone who has learned how to pray, and to pray in silence, learns not to respond to people who don't show in their speech the sense of mystery.

In expounding his view, Burrell used the image of a therapist and a healthy personality. The therapist knows a healthy personality when he sees one, and he can give some general characteristics of healthy personalities, but if he is pressed, he will finally reach a point where he must say that he cannot give any more reasons but must simply say that he knows this man to be healthy. He is involved in an interpretative circle and at some point he will have to stop trying to articulate his criteria and simply display them.

James Ross would not accept this. He saw no reason why criteria should not be given for a healthy personality. And if criteria could be given on a first level, there was no reason why they should not be given on a second or on a third.

Donald Evans suggested that Burrell's position amounted to a form of fideism. Analysis often purports to give a neutral account of language, but actually it turns out to conceal some personal position, for instance a certain brand of Christianity. There is no authority in the analysis itself. The analytic approach is useful in clarifying what positions people are holding but it does not enable you to choose between positions. If Burrell objects that the desire for a general scheme of explanation is perverse, that simply leaves you with a personal existentialist appeal—How does this language or that scheme illuminate my experience?

Michael Novak again ended this part of the discussion with the mediating suggestion that there might not be so strong an opposition between Ogden and Burrell as appeared. The order of prayer represents the order of belief and the order of living precedes the order of thinking. The final criterion in these matters is what a man can show you, and he has to show you out of his own life. There is a reciprocal relation between theory and action. Theory sometimes leads to conversions in the way we live, while on the other hand (as William James said) you usually act first and then ask, "What must I believe to be acting this way?" Ogden was right to begin with existential faith, but he ought to dwell longer on this level, for you can touch all kinds of men by talking of this. And he should not take a science as his model for theology, he should take ethics, a set of attractions or "to be dones."

3. The Morality of Belief

In his paper, Van Harvey described himself as an alienated theologian, as much a doubter as a believer, a straggler who followed the Israelites on their pilgrimage, picking up the crumbs of the manna, and warming himself at the outer edges of their campfires. He felt that his alienation was a function of the morality of knowledge which has come to dominate the consciousness of the Western intellectual: skepticism against unfounded assertions, suspicion of irrational authority, the appeal to evidence, the careful qualification of one's claims. It was on this question of the morality of knowledge, or more specifically the morality of belief, that the discussion tended to focus.

Paul van Buren began by posing two questions to Van Harvey. Why should the alienated theologian be envious of the subjective certitude of the believer? Is this certitude not ruled out by the very morality of belief which the alienated theologian acknowledges? Should people have a blessed assurance which goes against that morality of belief? And secondly, how can the alienated theologian want the Israelites to go on in their misguided ways?

Harvey's reply was that he did not envy the Israelites their certitude about their second-order theological affirmations. But presumably these second-order affirmations were derived from some religious experience which at least some of the Israelites had had, and which the alienated theologian had not had.

This distinction between a first-order language which immediately described our personal experience and a second-order language which was interpretative and explanatory drew a protest from Ian Barbour. He insisted that all language, even in science, is theory-laden. Even first-order, I-Thou language is not uninterpreted but is simply an alternative set of terms. There is no way in which you can escape categories that have metaphysical implications. First-order language is really an alternative interpretative scheme, and one, moreover, which is incompatible with some other schemes.

Harvey would have none of this. I go with Buber, he said. We use first-order (I-Thou) discourse along with a variety of second-order languages which operate as explanatory hypotheses.

Quite a variety of people sought to offer Van Harvey help with his problem of alienation, but it turned out that Harvey had examined and rejected most of the possibilities beforehand. Frederick Ferré, for instance, suggested that he might think of himself not as a straggler but as a scout, as one who was exploring the possibilities of the religion of the future, though he recognized that there were some features of the paper which suggested that Harvey was not altogether ready for the future. For instance, he agreed with John Henry Newman in treating the

proposition "There may be a God" with far more seriousness
than the proposition "A murder has just been committed in
Japan." A really modern person, Ferré suggested, would find
that human cruelty would hurt more than the question of God's
existence. Harvey agreed. That's why I don't regard myself as a
scout, he said, for I do have Newman's problem.

Charles Scott offered Harvey another way out of his alienation—that he should simply drop the problem of theism and
center on what he found attractive in certain types of religious
experience, for his paper did focus on experience rather than on
God. Harvey replied that there was a psychological reason why
he could not do that: he read books by people such as Ogden
and Ross and he was well aware that if he could just get rid of
some hesitations, he could settle for a panentheism of a kind,
and that this would be perfectly compatible with everything he
has said. I respect people like Quine, he added. I find it hard to
say that metaphysics is dead, and I am quite open to the possibility that some great metaphysician may come along who will
solve some of these problems and give us again a metaphysical
vision.

Harvey's third comforter was Kai Neilsen who offered him
some conceptual therapy. There seem to be three possibilities
for a believer, he said: metaphysics, fideism, and religious experience. The mistake is to set these three over against one another, for none of them will stand alone. For instance, C. B.
Martin has shown that religious experience alone will get you
nowhere. However, if you take the three together, as three
strands in a single argument, it might help to make sense. It is
true that you cannot try to believe, but you can take a leap of
faith from religious experience to some second-order explanation.
And if you ask how a theologian is to decide between competing metaphysical claims, the answer might be that as a man
of faith he can take a proposition which has the logical status
of an experimental hypothesis, but take it *de fide*. On the basis

of your religious experience you could even accept a hypothesis that is not as strong as others.

James Ross urged Harvey to accept this and argued that he had already conceded the main points: that a metaphysical hypothesis about God might be plausible and that some religious experience might tip the scale in its favor. Harvey admitted that he had in fact taken that way once under the influence of F. R. Tennant, but his problem now was that the option that attracted him was more panentheistic or Spinozistic than traditionally orthodox.

Next to try was Michael Novak, who agreed that Harvey showed a right instinct in calling himself a straggler and not a scout, but he had two diagnoses of Harvey's complaint: first, that he was too Protestant; second, that he was too rationalistic. While Protestants have placed more emphasis on the individual than Catholics do, there is also among them a spontaneous loyalty to one single tradition. Catholics are more ready to recognize diversities within the tradition, such as Francis, Augustine, and Paul. Not only so, but when you ask about the continuity of tradition, they would not claim any strict continuity over the generations but only analogies between one generation and another. On the second point, he argued that Harvey's "morality of knowledge" put too much weight upon opinions and arguments. We are coming to an end, he said, of this kind of morality of knowledge and the sign of it is the fact that the universities of the West, which have been founded on it, are in trouble at a deep level. Kai Nielsen seemed to agree with this and said that though he thought himself a child of the eighteenth century, he had to admit that its morality of knowledge was not enough. But it was Carl Armbruster who attacked Harvey's view of the morality of knowledge most strongly. It seemed to him an outmoded Puritanical code. The notion that a man does not have a right to things he can't pay for seems hopelessly old-fashioned in this day of guaranteed annual wages.

And the idea that we cannot have beliefs that we can't account for seems equally archaic. Harvey's Puritanical code may be an appropriate model for a scientific laboratory, but life is bigger and sloppier than a laboratory.

Harvey's reply on this point was to confess himself also a child of the eighteenth century. I regret the passing of the achievements of the eighteenth century, he said. The morality of knowledge which they established was one of the great rational achievements of the West. I like rigorous philosophy. It will be a sad day when we lose it, and if we have to talk vaguely, we should have good reasons for talking vaguely. One ought not to indulge in subjectivism. It may be the morality of knowledge that makes me a straggler, but I learned this morality among the Israelites and it makes me wary of Christian apologetics which become sneaky and irrelevant.

Why, then, asked Heinrich Ott, did Harvey choose as the motto for his paper this quotation from Wittgenstein about running against the boundaries of language? The later Wittgenstein deliberately ran against the boundaries of language, and surely it would change things greatly for the alienated theologian to recognize that there is another type of language than referential?

Harvey's reply was to say that he had indeed been impressed by Wittgenstein's notebooks and Wittgenstein's apparent religious experience. No doubt such things do change your way of looking at the world, but it seemed to him an incredible reading of Wittgenstein to drop the idea of reference altogether. Language will always have some referential character, and the words "I believe" and "I know" refer to things on which we can give arguments and hope to get agreements. How do you pass from data to conclusions except by appeal to warrants?

And so, despite the efforts of his friends, Van Harvey ended the discussion still an alienated theologian.

4. The Future of Philosophical Theology

The future of philosophical theology was the title of the Consultation as a whole, and naturally it became the main topic of the closing session. On the whole, the Consultants tended to line up on this issue much as they had on the question whether metaphysics was constructive or analytic. Those who saw metaphysics as essentially constructive expected the future of philosophical theology to be recognizably like its past. Those who favored an analytic metaphysics foresaw a philosophical theology which would be more like literary criticism.

There were some fresh ideas, such as Frederick Ferré's suggestion that the next generation of philosophical theologians would be so accustomed to the use of psychedelic drugs that they would be ready to use them to control the manna for which Israelites throughout the centuries had had to wait patiently. His contention was that drugs can induce experiences which are indistinguishable from mystical experiences, and he anticipated the use of drugs in retreat houses under the auspices of the church. Van Harvey disagreed with this. While sometimes drug-induced experiences can be introduced into a life-style, more often they cannot, and far from promoting the "nameless gratitude" characteristic of religious experience, they are a way of copping out.

Thomas Munson had a different suggestion, that the Consultation had limited itself very notably to Western religion and Western philosophy, and that the wider perspective introduced by the History of Religions might have something to teach us and might suggest to us new ways of tackling our own problems. There was no time, however, to discuss this topic.

The main supporters of a new style of philosophical theology were Paul van Buren, David Burrell, Frederick Sontag, and Charles Scott.

Paul van Buren saw philosophical theology becoming in the

future a blend of literary criticism and psychology. There would
continue to be a minority of people such as Ogden and Ross
who would perpetuate the older traditions, but the emphasis
would be on experience. Frederick Sontag agreed that the focus
would be religious experience and the epistemology of religious
knowledge, and that there would be a backing away from the
constructive task. But he thought it would be a backing away
toward philosophy of religion rather than literary criticism. However, he had to admit that he found students interested in constructive attempts and conceded that they might be right.
Charles Scott took the view that metaphysics is not viable just
now and that this is a time to withdraw in the face of new elements in our culture in order to find out what will enliven
theology again. Lastly, David Burrell reiterated his view that the
future of philosophical theology must be analytic and reflective
rather than constructive. He was even willing to "recant" the
opening comments in his paper because they seemed to him
now to go too far in the direction of exhibiting a substantive
position on God. He did feel committed to philosophy as a
search for criteria, but the manner in which criteria function is
ingredient in our idea of what a criterion is. The meaning of
criteria is illustrated in their use.

In opposition to all this were those who defended a more
traditional kind of philosophical theology. If philosophical theology becomes literary criticism, said Kai Nielsen, it is dead. One
has to try to do what Ogden and Harvey are trying to do, because at the heart of Christianity and Judaism are certain puta-
tive truth claims. The appeal to religious experience is dubious
if it does not enable one to determine these truth claims. The
word "God" is referential, and religious experience doesn't take
care of this. Neither is the appeal to special criteria for special
areas of experience a helpful one. There were once special
criteria for talk about fairies and gremlins, but that does not
prove that the whole project may not have been wrong. As long
as the question of God remains doubtful we must come back

to it obsessively. Joe Bracken agreed, and thought that the defenders of a new style of philosophical theology were asking too much. You can argue with a man on a rational basis, he added, but if a man says to you that you have to live out his philosophy in order to know whether it is right, then there is no basis for argument.

James Ross naturally took the same view, and urged philosophical theologians to be constructive. There is a traditional obligation for theology to construct and not merely to analyze, he said. Of course, philosophers can analyze and theologians can too, but theologians must also construct. They must put up or shut up. The constructive aspects of philosophical theology have been too narrowly conceived, and theologians cannot leave people's legitimate expectations unanswered. Try something constructive! The worst that can happen to you is that you fail. Even Schleiermacher and James tried to construct, and the whole history of philosophical theology suggests that it can be done if not correctly, at least successfully.

Finally, Schubert Ogden added his arguments. He thought of philosophical theology not as systematic or constructive theology, but along the lines of the old natural theology. He agreed with Kai Nielsen that the appeal to a variety of language games was a dangerous one. It brought the temptation to settle too comfortably into the view that religion is merely one form of life among others, to accept metaphysical neutralism and to avoid questions of criteria. This is a temptation to be resisted. On the other hand, we should avoid the imperialism of the positivists, who point to the problematic character of the religious form of life. We must call in question the criteria by which they make this judgment. We cannot avoid the discussion of criteria. And while it is true that we ought to be constructive, we need not apologize for occupying ourselves with questions of method. It is part of our task, and in discussing criteria we are discussing the question of God.

The issue that divides us most is whether the model for

philosophical theology should be literary criticism or science. On this point, Ogden was willing to concede that theology isn't everything and that life is indeed much richer than theology. But his last word was that there is no incompatibility between living and thinking.

Between these two positions there was not much middle ground. Van Harvey did not so much mediate as take up a cross-bench position. He would not commit himself to either side. On the one hand, he said that he did not want to make his own malaise normative and was open to the possibility that a metaphysical vision of enormous power might again come into existence. On the other hand, he felt that as of now metaphysics was in disarray and there was a low market value for constructive theology. After all, what does it mean to be constructive? Why construct a palace in which one does not live? The task of philosophical theology is not to build empty palaces but to aid the church in bringing men to faith. We should recognize the speculative nature of metaphysics, be more reticent, and not claim to know too much.

Michael Novak was one of the few to make an attempt at mediation. He felt that people were posing the differences too sharply, and were overlooking an intermediate position. What is critical, he said, is the middle position between wonder and concept. Both claims, that we have to deal with experience and that the task of philosophical theology is constructive, are true. What we are constructing is an account of the way human beings have to view the world in order to act in certain ways. In our culture we should not be trying to do philosophical theology in the classical mode. Nowadays, even in science, we have come to see that our theories are a reflection of ourselves. How much more must this be true in theology!

The other mediator was Heinrich Ott. He confessed himself puzzled about the two options for metaphysics sponsored by Ogden and Burrell respectively. He himself was inclined to reject general metaphysics without dispensing with metaphysical interests. My general approach, he said, is hermeneutical. I begin both with that primal awareness which we have in personal experience and which is in no need of justification, and with the claims of revelation. The problem is how to bring these two starting points together.

My question to Ogden is: What do you mean by "our common faith"? Do you mean the common awareness which man has of himself and which is the condition of both authenticity and inauthenticity? If so, why do you interpret this awareness as faith—it makes the transition to metaphysics too easy.

My question to Burrell is: You see the task of philosophical theology as analytic and therapeutic, but do you not agree that there is more—a constructive task?

Dr. Ott's questions went unanswered, at least in the formal discussions, as the Consultation came to its end. As the Chairman had predicted, it did not result in agreement, but it did produce a greater understanding of the issues before us.

back to the point where he bumped up against the boundaries of analysis and had to recognize that fact: at the unique, the underivable, the presence of form (*das Gestalthafte*)—I would say: the presence of meaning (*das Sinnhafte*)—which belongs essentially to the aesthetic experience. "I may draw you a face. Then at another time I draw another face. You say: 'That's not the same face'—but you can't say whether the eyes are closer together, or mouth longer, or anything of this sort. 'It looks different somehow.' This is enormously important for all philosophy." [11] Thus the aesthetic established its own sphere of experience and language beyond the mechanically or "psycho-mechanically" explainable. Wittgenstein appears to have still more in view than merely the aesthetic in the narrower sense. The aesthetic as a common and easily observable experience in a certain sense only opens for him the gate to the other, the nonderivable reality which is not reducible to the simplest elements. And for him the whole domain of the psychic belongs to that latter realm, as his critique of Freud shows. By way of analysis, Wittgenstein arrived at the threshold of that which cannot be analyzed further.

But at this threshold difficulties arise for anyone who has tried to think along this far and wants now to think further. Here one seems to find only the irrational, the arbitrary: aesthetic experiences simply are what they are. And the forms of life and the corresponding language games within whose horizons the aesthetic experiences occur simply are as they are. For instance, "Wearing blue or green pants may in a certain society mean a lot, but in another society it may not mean anything." [12] Apparently nothing more can be said of the aesthetic experience in its always specific character than it *is* so experienced. "One asks such a question as 'What does this remind me of?' or one says of a piece of music: 'This is like some sentence, but what sentence is it like?' Various things are suggested; one thing, as you say, clicks. What does it mean, it 'clicks'? Does it do anything you can compare to the noise of a click? Is there the ringing of a bell, or something comparable?" [13]

Here the question arises whether we are really unable to think further. If, for example, we experience and judge the same thing from the viewpoint of different forms of life, of different cultures (I think here not of blue or green pants, but rather, for instance, of a landscape or a substantial work of art), is there then no communication between the two worlds except when someone arbitrarily leaves the one form of life and enters the other? Are the forms of life and their language games separated from each other, isolated? Or does something which establishes a possibility of comparison, a communicability of experiences between different worlds, forms of life, cultural contexts, and language games grow up from the thing itself, that is, from the object of the aesthetic experience or some other experience in the realm of the unique, the irreducible? If I find a particular landscape beautiful, a particular sort of human behavior noble, and another from the point of view of his form of life finds the same landscape ugly, the same behavior vulgar—can we then no longer communicate with each other?

Or how does it happen—this question too leads in the same direction—that new forms of life and language games arise or that forms of life and language games modify themselves? Is there rational comprehension only within the given framework, within the given rules of the game? Or is there a more primordial thinking? Here it will be helpful to follow the lead to which Martin Heidegger's guiding concept of truth as a-letheia, as nonconcealment, points. "Truth" in this sense means "clearing," the emerging into the nonconcealed, the showing of itself, and in this area thought and speech for the first time become possible.

> That which clears lasts insofar as it clears. We call its act of clearing "the clearing" [as a clearing in a forest]. What belongs to it, how it happens and where, remain for fur-

ther thought. That which clears makes things shine, and frees these shining things so that they may appear to us. The free is the realm of non-concealment. . . . Why is it so that one stubbornly rejects any consideration of whether the correlation of subject and object does not move in something which grants to the object and its objectivity, to the subject and its subjectivity their essence in the first place, and which, anterior to this essence, grants them the realm of their correlation? [14]

"That which belongs to it [to the clearing], how it happens and where, remain for further thought," says Heidegger. The question does in fact remain open and needs further thought. Wittgenstein for his part has opened it for us in that he pushed forward to the boundaries of an analytical understanding of language and of a positivistic understanding of reality and made this boundary concretely visible with respect to the phenomenon of the aesthetic experience and of the aesthetic judgment. The question that must now be asked can be put in the following form: How, in the experience of reality, do we again and again acquire a possibility of speaking? Therefore: How does an area of speaking clear up, how does it constitute itself? What actually happens here? How can new language games and forms of life thus arise? And how is communication between the language games possible—transposition (*Über-setzung*) from the one into the other? For *a-letheia*, clearing, constitutes communication. *A-letheia*, "clearing," therefore means simultaneously the "possibility of communication." We must be all the more willing, if we ask about communication between different worlds, different contexts, to risk that step back behind the given game rules into the more primordial realm of clearing, which sponsors communication.

This is the philosophical problem. Its theological relevance is clear, especially if we reflect back to Wittgenstein's aporetic passages on religious speaking which we quoted. "How, in the experience of reality, do we again and again acquire a possibility of speaking?" For theology, that means "How, out of the specific experience of faith, does one attain to the articulation (*Sprach-Werdung*) of the faith: in prayer, in witness, in theology itself?" *Where is that astonishing link* where speech emerges from experience? And what is it exactly which occurs at that point?

I was invited to deliver a programmatic speech. Now, if you set up a program, you are not obliged to accomplish it all at once. I frankly admit that I have no solutions for the specific paradigmatic problems I am posing here. But I was asked to give at least some hints as to how I think it is possible to approach these problems. That is what I am going to do:

For our first problem, I assume that we will have to examine the points where language arises. So, for instance, Martin Buber has interpreted the name of God "YHWH" as originally being "*Jahwu*," an enthusiastic cry which wants to say, "Oh, He!" This would be an original disclosure, an articulation (*Sprach-Werdung*), a sudden realizing and response. One would have to investigate what thereby is disclosed for man, that is, how through this sudden realization a new light is shed on his existence, giving so to speak new colors to all or to many phenomena of life. This sort of investigation might lead us farther.

2. The second problem concerns the *essence of the social*. We live in a time in which theology is rediscovering the social dimension. This discovery is indeed essential for theology, for how could one speak honestly concerning the church, which is itself a social phenomenon, concerning the Spirit of God, who according to our faith inspires the church, concerning the task of the church in human society and concerning its chances of fulfilling this task without a realistic knowledge of the social phenomena?

It seems to me that the investigation of social phenomena today urgently needs a philosophical clarification—especially if the social sciences are beginning to play a role in the process of forming the political will, and if their diagnosis thus begins

NOTES ON CONTRIBUTORS

ROBERT A. EVANS was born in El Dorado, Kansas, in 1937 and studied at Yale University, the University of Basel, and received his Th.D. from Union Theological Seminary, New York. He is the author of *Intelligible and Responsible Talk About God* and *Belief and the Counter Culture*, to be published in the fall of 1971. He is Assistant Professor of Philosophical Theology at McCormick Theological Seminary.

SCHUBERT M. OGDEN was born in Cincinnati, Ohio, in 1928 and studied at Ohio Wesleyan University and the University of Chicago where he received his Ph.D. He is the author of *Christ Without Myth* and *The Reality of God*. He is University Professor of Theology at the Divinity School, University of Chicago.

DAVID B. BURRELL, C.S.C., was born in Akron, Ohio, in 1933 and studied at the University of Notre Dame, the Gregorian University, Rome, and received his Ph.D. from Yale University. He is the editor of Bernard Lonergan's *Verbum: Word and Ideas in Aquinas* and "Knowing as a Personal and Passionate Quest: A Study of C. S. Peirce" in *American Philosophy and the Future*. He is Assistant Professor in Philosophy at the University of Notre Dame.

VAN A. HARVEY was born in Hankow, China, in 1926 and studied at Occidental College and Yale University where he received his Ph.D. He is the author of *The Historian and the Believer* and *A Handbook of Theological Terms*. He is Professor of Religious Thought at the University of Pennsylvania.

HEINRICH OTT was born in Basel, Switzerland, in 1929 and studied at the University of Marburg and the University of Basel where he received his D. Theol. He is the author of *Denken und Sein, Wirklichkeit und Glaube* (2 vols.) and *Theology and Preaching*. He is Professor of Systematic Theology at the University of Basel.

DONALD M. MATHERS was born in Monifieth, Scotland, in 1921 and studied at the University of St. Andrews, Union Theological Seminary in New York, and received his Ph.D. from Columbia University. He is the author of *The Word and the Way* and *A New Look at Belief*. He is Principal and Professor of Systematic Theology and Philosophy of Religion at Queen's Theological College, Kingston, Ontario.